D

To my mother:
I can't imagine the feelings of having a child who is a
runaway. If you had not been such a stabilizing force through
all the troubled years, I would have, most surely, been lost.

To my wife and our children:
For continuing to join with me in our mutual healing
process. I know it's tough to have a husband/father/
stepfather who still messes up so much. Thanks for your
patience and commitment to not give up on me.

To Lance:
Not only one of the best pool players I've ever known, but
also the best friend I could ever imagine. We've gone through
many trials on our journeys together … and you still take me
as I am.

To all the street people I've encountered who were often so
real and open with their feelings. I have learned much from
them.

ACKNOWLEDGEMENT

There are always many people who have influence and contribute in many ways to the completion of a book of this nature. I want to recognize two of them.

Cover Art By:
Laurent H. Dillon Jr. Renaissance Inc.
Artist Extraordinaire ...and a good friend.

To my Outstanding Executive Assistant, Colette, thank you for your patience and understanding while working with both the Street Kid and the Therapist. You're Awesome!

TABLE OF CONTENTS

The Street Kid Chapters

The Therapist Chapters

THE CONFLICT

❦

«Hey, I want to go shoot pool.»

"Yeah, why don't you? It'll be good to get away a little … But we need to work on the book today."

«Who's the 'we'?»

"Well, *I* am writing about *you*, the 'street kid' … the teenage runaway … pretending to be an adult. And of course I am writing about your journey of self-discovery, through failure into a life with meaning and purpose. How's that sound?"

«Sounds like you're pretending to be the 'therapist' … you know, the Ph.D.!»

"But I *am* the 'therapist' … the Ph.D.."

«Not without me you're not. Without me you'd probably wind up as a stuffy, book-smart college professor. Anyway, I don't want to work today.»

"Come on, it'll be fun! You can tell me one of your stories … tell me again about the escape. I like that one."

«Okay, you win. You remember it happened one time when I was on the run and …»

❧

The conversation inside my head … today. Just the ruminations of the "street kid" and the "therapist" to see which one is going to be in control … today.

The Street Kid

He is always *pretending* to be something that he is not—like
an adult on the streets of skid row when he was only thirteen
years old, or a college professor, or a family therapist, even
though he is *always thirteen*.

He feels that he can't be *real*, or he'll be rejected. He feels
that he just doesn't fit in.

The Therapist

He wants to help the street kid believe in himself and realize
that all the failures of the past (and future) produce a kind
of *wisdom*, with *valuable insights* that can be helpful to the
therapist as he counsels others with similar issues.

He also secretly wants the street kid to *play* more often,
so the therapist can get away from the pressure of being
good all the time. He just knows that while it would be great
to get away, the street kid doesn't always play fair … and can
get in a lot of trouble.

∽

There is a symphony of voices inside my head SHOUTING
their wisdom from the lessons of my past.

The Street Kid

Pool Hustler   Salesman   Pastor
Student   Parent
Clinical Director   Food Server   Bouncer
Professor   Addict
Bartender   Child Care Worker   Fundraiser

The Therapist

"E PLURIBUS UNUM…"
"…ONE OUT OF MANY"

For those who can relate, we all have an amalgamation of
beings within us.
This is their journey … and mine.

"DOWNTOWN"

When you're alone
And life is making you lonely
You can always go downtown
When you've got worries,
All the noise and the hurry
Seems to help, I know, downtown
Sung by Petula Clark

I like alleys. I like the cushion from the noise of the city. I like watching the people rushing past the alleys along the sidewalk. I like the coolness of the shadows on a hot day. I like the nooks and crannies offered by the back entrances to nameless buildings.

But most of all, in the alleys, I like hiding.

I like being able to watch without being seen. If anybody looks too closely and sees the real me, he or she will discover that I'm just a runaway living on the streets, afraid of going home.

It feels like I have been a *runaway* all of my life. I started running away from home at the age of eleven, after my parents divorced, but the desire to escape continued long into my adult life. The feeling of wanting to run continues even now. My life is mostly good, but at any moment something may trigger the impulse to run. It could be a smell, an experience, a long-forgotten memory, a feeling that I've done something wrong and am in trouble again. The feeling is often brief and I can resist it, but sometimes the desire to run away is almost overwhelming. The emotional defenses that have taken years to develop can fall apart in an instant, and I suddenly feel the combination of excitement and fear as I move toward the self-destructive and dangerous behavior of running away.

I also feel like I have been a *failure* all of my life. Not that I didn't have successes later in life, but even then I was driven by a fear of failure ... afraid that if anyone found out who the real me was, he or she would reject me and I would be exposed as a failure anyway. Many teachers, probation officers, counselors, etc. have said to me, "You have so much potential." To me, this was only an indictment of the obvious: that I was failing to be what *they* wanted. I felt that while I could not live up to their expectations, I could certainly live up to my own.

I was a failure—a dropout, a street kid who really didn't fit in the world of success or happiness.

In my mind, "happiness" was often connected to the role that I played while a runaway as a young teenager on the streets of Seattle. Throughout my life, people have responded with sympathy and concern when they learned that I was a runaway on the streets, but it has always been a struggle to explain that I was not a runaway by chance; I was a runaway by choice. I lived on the streets because I wanted to be there … and often still do!

The street has a life of its own. In Seattle, standing on the corner of First Avenue and Yesler Way facing north, the small cobblestone triangular park called Pioneer Square with its Alaskan totem pole and cast-iron and glass pergola in the middle of the street is on the right just across First Avenue. The waterfront is to the left a couple of blocks down on Yesler toward Alaskan Way. Two blocks south on First Avenue are the missions that offer a church service, a meal, and a bed—in that order, because you have to sit through the church service before you can receive a hot meal and a warm bed. From the missions, Jackson Street runs east from First Avenue up past the train station toward the ghetto, with Chinatown to the south.

This entire area was called Skid Road, named for the original place where loggers would skid logs down the hill to Elliot Bay. But, as in many other cities, it simply became known as "skid row," to describe the long slide down to the bottom of life that the residents had descended before winding up there.

While it was certainly a destination of pain and misery for a lot of people, it was much different for a thirteen-year-old boy, a runaway pretending to be a man. For me, it was a magical place of excitement and possibilities. During the day, there was a lot of activity, with cars and cabs and buses taking businesspeople in suits with briefcases to various places of apparent importance. The rush of the people on the sidewalks and the sounds of the traffic were rivaled only by the sounds coming from the activity on the waterfront. The cargo ships and the tugboats, the foghorns from the ferries, the smell of fish from the canneries—all added to the sense of vibrancy that was downtown Seattle during the daytime.

At night, there was also a lot of activity, but of a completely different kind. First Avenue up to Pike Street was filled with streetwalkers and pimps, dope dealers, and small-time hustlers, who huddled in the doorways and on the sidewalks in front of the pawn shops, flophouse hotels, and skid row taverns. The nighttime on the streets became a place of adventure. A place of potential, offering different kinds of action. A place of "connections" that could hide the reality of being a young, vulnerable teenager who had run away from home.

∞

The streets represented a calling to a new life. I was six foot three at thirteen and six foot six at fourteen, and was able to pass for an adult. To be an adult meant that I was free. On the streets I made "friends." These were people who knew me ... and protected me.

I remember hanging out in a bar called No Place, which was on the corner of Washington and Occidental. I had hung out there on several previous occasions, but this time when I went in, there was a beat cop from the Seattle Police

Department just inside. He looked at me and questioned my age. At that moment, the bartender looked over and said to the cop, "I know him; he's all right." After that I was in; that cop never bothered me again.

On the streets, I lived a life of fantasy. I was an adult, not a troubled young teenager who didn't want to go home. On the streets, I had no responsibility, no studies or homework, no authority figures to tell me what to do, or not do. On the streets, I could escape it all. On the streets, I didn't have any fear of physical abuse, rejection, or alienation. On the streets, I became somebody else—somebody who didn't have any problems, somebody who didn't have any pain.

Often as an adult, when things would go wrong or when I would feel pressure to perform in my job or in relationships, my mind would pull me toward wanting to escape it all. During these times, I just wanted to run away again, and the fantasy would take me to the streets of Seattle. I wanted to go to the waterfront again. I wanted to smell the clam chowder and fish and chips at Ivar's Fish Bar on Pier 54. I wanted to walk around aimlessly, feeling the freedom again as I listened to the sounds of the city and watched the people.

However, I often could not actually go back to Seattle, so I escaped into the memories of life as a street kid. The street kid was the underlying self-image that I felt when I could no longer keep up the pretense of trying to fit in the real world. The street kid told me that I was still just a pretender, hiding among the real people, and that if I would just run away I would be safe.

A failure of course but safe … and free.

༄

I remember standing on a sidewalk in front of a café called the Skidroad Beanery on Washington Street near First Avenue. I was hungry, and the smell of bean soup spilled out into the street, making my mouth water as I imagined tasting the fine cuisine.

I remember thinking, *What am I doing here anyway? Three years ago I was a Cub Scout. Now I am a «twenty-two-year-old adult» who is homeless on the streets. I'm cold, I'm lonely.*

What was that girl's name in the dance class at the junior high? She was just left over like me after everybody else had paired off; it was just her and me. I can't believe she didn't want to dance with me because I looked like an old man. It's not my fault that I'm this tall. Why do I need to learn how to dance anyway, especially in seventh grade? I'm glad I don't have to put up with that anymore. How long ago was that anyway? Weeks? Feels like years.

That's my old life. I need to forget my old life. I've got more important things to think about … I need to go bum some money and get myself some of that soup. That will be great; I can't wait to taste it. Boy, if the kids at Jane Addams Junior High could see me now, I bet they would wish they were here enjoying this freedom. It doesn't get any better than this!

∽

On the streets, I didn't want to think about bad times or the feelings of being hurt, so I made up a new identity. I picked a name that I could remember easily but didn't sound like an alias. I became Richard Boyle, twenty-two years old, single, and looking for excitement.

I met a girl at a small lunch café on First Avenue between Pine and Pike streets. She was nice and good looking and friendly. She said she was seventeen but that she liked older guys. I of course was a lonely thirteen-year-old, but in my new identity, I was twenty-two, which she seemed to like. We talked about going somewhere together ... maybe to Ivar's to get some fish and chips, and feed the seagulls. It sounded like we had a lot in common, and I thought I might actually have found a friend ... and who knows, maybe even a girlfriend.

Then an older man walked in. He was at least forty and looked like he had money and style. He gave her money to play the jukebox and then started dancing with her. He bent down and whispered something in her ear. She returned to me and said, "Sorry, I've gotta go. Maybe I'll see you around." She walked out with the old guy, and just like that, she was gone forever.

I remember thinking, *So what's the deal? The girl in dance class didn't want me because I looked too old. This one doesn't want me because I don't look old enough. Who cares ... it's all just a game. I'd rather be by myself anyway. I think I'll go down to Ivar's and bum some money from an old lady, someone that won't mind what my age is or what I look like!*

∾

When I wasn't running away to the streets of downtown Seattle, I tried to reconnect with my dad in Ashland, Oregon. Even though he didn't call or try to see me, I was sure that it was his new wife who kept him from doing so. I knew that if I could just spend some time with him, he would realize that it was a mistake to have moved from Arkansas.

The end to this nightmare would be to get my parents back together. If we could only get back to Arkansas, everything would be happy again!

On one of those trips to Oregon, I got caught and was placed in the Juvenile Detention Center in Medford, because I was "out of parental control." The kid in the next room, named Carl, happened to be from Arkansas. In the evenings, we talked through the electric outlet in the wall between us. He wanted to run back home, and we talked about how good it would be once we got there.

One afternoon, the staff who supervised the detention center took a group of us kids outside the fence for a work detail. Carl whispered to me, "This is our chance; as soon as his back is turned, we'll run." Before we could plan how to meet up if we got separated or even which way to go, the supervisor (who was a nice guy who treated us well and trusted us enough to let us work outside) told us that he had to go back inside for something.

Carl said, "Now," dropped his shovel, and took off running. At the time, I was thirteen years old, six foot three, uncoordinated, and often felt like I could hardly walk straight let alone run. I took off running after my fellow escapee, but within a couple of minutes, he was gone and out of sight.

I started heading toward the bushes down by the river, putting some distance between myself and the detention center, when suddenly I heard two loud noises that sounded like gunshots. "They are shooting at us!" my mind screamed. I dove head-first into the nearest bush.

The bush turned out to be full of little thorns, which tore my clothing and skin, but I didn't care. I knelt there, frozen in fear, wondering if I had been seen as I disappeared into the bushes. The evening sun was starting to go down, and I reasoned with myself that if I could just wait until dark, I could start moving again.

After about half an hour, I heard footsteps. As the footsteps came closer to me, I heard a faint clinking sound like metal against metal. I suddenly realized what it must be … the police had seen me after all and were searching the bushes near me. The clinking sounds, which grew louder as they approached my hiding place, were from the keys or handcuffs on their belts!

After what seemed like a couple of hours, the footsteps came within a few feet of me. I just couldn't take it anymore ... and jumped up and burst out of the bushes yelling, "Okay, you've got me!"

In doing so, I almost ran over the most startled cow I had ever seen in my life. I felt instant relief, followed by the exhilaration of still being free. Within a few moments, I also felt completely exhausted ... and discouraged. It all just seemed to represent the futility of my life—another split-second decision to run away, being too clumsy to run quickly, finding myself alone with nowhere to go, and now the humiliation of being held down frozen in fear by a cow (and her cowbell) that was smarter than I was; at least she had chosen a path near the river where the grass was good, and it made sense that *she* was there!

I lay down and slept for a little while, and when I woke up, it was dark. I felt a little better and decided to walk back toward the highway, using the fruit tree orchard as cover so I wouldn't be seen. I finally got up the nerve to try hitchhiking. I reasoned that I would try it with just one car and see what happened. As the headlights approached, I stuck out my thumb and was shocked to see the entire car light up.

Red lights, spotlights, and interior lights came on as the car screeched to a halt. As the car door on the passenger side

opened, I saw the words "Oregon State Police" and heard
a voice say, "Get down on the ground!" He handcuffed
me, and as he put me in the back of the patrol car, he said,
"We've been waiting; we knew you'd turn up sooner or later."

When I got back to the detention center, Carl was there
too. He said he'd been caught after he'd been gone about
fifteen minutes. He said he was running across a field when
he heard what he thought were gunshots and looked over to
see a patrol car parked by the highway with cops waving at
him. We never found out if they actually fired a gun or not,
but whatever it was, it sure worked.

Neither of us got out of our rooms much after that,
and I had a lot of time to think about how stupid the whole
thing was.

❧

"Stupid? That's the understatement of the year …
or the lifetime."

"It sounded like a good idea at the time—live
and learn."

"I hope so!"

❧

After a couple of weeks, I was released to go live with my dad in Ashland, Oregon, after promising that I wouldn't try to run away again.

My dad was a music professor at Southern Oregon College. He had a nice house where he lived with his new family, and for a while, things were okay with me there. I was in the eighth grade, made a couple of friends, and actually began to think that my problems were over.

Then one day I got into a fight with my dad's new wife. She told my dad to call the probation officer to come get me. When the probation officer came to the house later that evening, my dad told him he had called my mother and they had decided to let me try to live with her and my little sister in Seattle again. But the juvenile court would have to agree.

I was allowed to stay at my dad's house until the court papers could be filed, but I had to promise that I wouldn't cause any more problems. Just before the probation officer left that night, he took my dad aside and I overheard him say, "I've never actually worked with your son directly, but I know his type, and you can forget about him because he'll spend the rest of his life behind bars."

A few days later, just before he put me on the bus going to Seattle, my dad told me that people weren't going to put up with my behavior anymore and further that he was "giving up" on me, because although he was still my father, he was not my "dad."

As I got on the bus, I thought, *Great ... I don't need a dad.* And even though I was going to try it again with my mom (who would always be there for me to do the best she could), I thought I didn't really need a mom either. I just needed to get back to Arkansas!

2

"SOMEWHERE OVER THE RAINBOW"

Someday I'll wish upon a star
And wake up where the clouds are far
Behind me.
Where troubles melt like lemon drops
Away above the chimney tops
That's where you'll find me
          Sung by Judy Garland

As a therapist, I've worked with a lot of kids (and adults too) who just wanted to get their lives back together, the way things were before the trauma happened. It doesn't seem to matter what the tragedy was—death, divorce, accident, or disease—they still wanted to get back to a time that seemed free from all the pain.

It doesn't even seem to matter if it makes sense or that reality and logic could never allow the same situation or circumstance to happen again. They still do everything they can to make it real once more in their lives. As a result, their thoughts and behaviors are often dominated by a false hope that drives their actions into increasing disorder and dysfunction, not because they want to be disruptive, but because their hopeless quest only furthers their alienation and isolation from the real world.

For instance, I worked with a woman in art therapy who drew a picture of herself as a nine-year-old girl standing on the porch, watching her father drive away for the last time, after her parents separated. She felt that she was closer to her father than her siblings were and that he would soon come back to rescue her from the family.

She related that she had that image stuck in her mind and still experienced the fantasy that he would drive up, even after many years, wrap his loving arms around her, and take her away from all the feelings of loss. He never did. His death was her primary motivation for seeking therapy. She knew he was gone, but she still wanted him to come back for her.

∽

In the events and circumstances leading to my being in the Juvenile Detention Center in Medford, Oregon, I wasn't trying to be a troublemaker; I just wanted to go home.

It was obvious that my home in Arkadelphia, Arkansas, didn't exist anymore. In fact in hindsight later as an adult, it became obvious that it probably wasn't the happy home that I always envisioned anyway. My parents likely had a dysfunctional relationship even in Arkansas. But at the age of thirteen (and even now sometimes), I wanted to go back and relive those "happy" times before the divorce and destruction that followed.

It's like watching a film of the airplane flying toward the World Trade Center on 9/11 and just for a fleeting moment wishing it wouldn't hit the building this time. We know that it doesn't make any sense, but just for a moment, the fantasy exists.

Childhood fantasies seem to go on forever. They take different forms and shapes, but nobody seems able to make them go away.

The past was so exciting but also so unattainable. The present was like a nightmare out of which I couldn't awaken. The future offered no hope for escape, leaving me trapped in an existence that I didn't want with nowhere to go but into darkness, alone and afraid.

So, I learned how to fake it. I didn't tell anybody my real feelings. I reasoned that if I didn't open up to anybody, even if they appeared to actually care, maybe they wouldn't see the real me ... maybe they wouldn't know that I was dumb, hurting, and lost.

The feeling that I was dumb came from my self-image. I remember my mom telling me that I had done poorly on achievement tests upon entering the seventh grade and the school recommended that I be placed back in sixth grade. My mom told them that I had always done well in school before and wondered if some other factor affected the scores. The school didn't think the tests could be wrong, but they allowed me to stay, at the insistence of my mother. I think my mom told me this to reassure me that I would not be held back, but to me, it just confirmed what I had begun to believe: I was too dumb to be there ... or anywhere.

In middle school and high school, I was often unable to pay attention in class because of the chaos in my life, but I just blamed myself. Later, as I progressed through higher education, I still had the feeling that I was pretending to fit in with true intellectuals; in my heart, I wasn't even close to their mental acuity.

When I finally went to college, I took a lot of classes that were designed to help me learn to eventually become a counselor to troubled kids and hurting family members. I felt that I was still hiding who I really was, and I didn't fake it so well in my first college attempt, getting a 0.0 grade point average at the end of the first quarter. At that time in my life, I felt driven to show people that I really was the failure that I had come to believe about myself.

❧

«What's up with that anyway? I mean, which one of us is responsible for blowing it that bad? A 0.0 grade point average?»

"Must be *your* fault; after all, I did much better the next time."

෴

Later, I had changed enough to fake it better and eventually finished my BA in psychology, sociology, and social work—a triple major to show how accomplished I had become. A master of education in counseling followed, and finally a doctor of philosophy in psychology. I was a Ph.D.!

But, all the way through my college studies and experiences, I was driven by a fear of failure. Underneath the facade that I showed to others, I had a dark secret, a secret that I didn't want anyone to know—I was still a failure in my heart.

∽

I remember talking to some of my classmates in the doctoral program; they seemed much smarter than I was. They knew things about academics that I had never even heard before. They often described abstract concepts that felt so far beyond me, I could only listen and nod my head. These people *belonged* in a doctoral program; I was in way over my head but afraid to quit because I couldn't allow the failure to fuel my self-destruction.

The classes and the professors constantly reinforced my subconscious belief that I *knew* I didn't belong, and if it ever became public, I would be drummed out of the university with the door shutting in a clanging sound that would only be rivaled by the memory of the steel door closing behind me in the detention center.

My primary secret that I was a failure was consistently being self-reinforced by my negative thoughts and behaviors in the choices I continued to make in the "real world." I remember sitting in a large classroom filled with doctoral students who were interacting with a world-renowned professor named Max Lerner from New York City. Max (as he liked to be called) had emphatically presented the question "What is it that DRIVES you?"

As my fellow students called out the forces that shaped their lives, Max wrote them on the board with connecting circles that made them appear as a living organism. He wrote "love, belonging, family, marriage, learning, sex," and a host of other wonderful things that motivated human beings to new heights.

I sat in silence, bewildered, because only one word kept reverberating through my simplistic mind. Finally when I could stand its echoing no more, I blurted out, "What about *self-destruction*?"

Max seemed to leap in my direction; he pointed his eighty-year-old finger at me and exclaimed, "Aha!" with more force in his voice than I had heard before.

I suddenly knew that I had blown it. I had exposed my secret to one of the world's most respected scholars, in front of all the students who really belonged there. I was horrified and humiliated. And then Max cried out with a plea, "Lord, don't take my demons from me, because then my angels will leave too!"

Max began a discussion on the need for harmony and balance between the dark and light in each of our lives. I didn't participate in the discussion, not wanting to reveal more than I had already, but I was aware of a tiny glimmer of hope from deep within. Maybe there was something I could gain from all the failure. Maybe there was something good that could be part of me that wasn't just fake. Maybe … maybe.

The next thought jolted me back to reality. Max and the real doctoral students were talking about balance and harmony. That certainly didn't apply to me! While I did have desires and impulses to do the right thing, and even to help people if I could, most of my desires were to run away from the responsibility, to escape from the needs of other people, and above all, to find something (even temporarily) that took away the fear, the turmoil, and the pain inside.

Part of me wanted to believe that I was capable of finding a balance between the light and dark forces that seemed so far apart in my inner world, but most certainly I had gone too far. I felt like Darth Vader in *Star Wars*; he may have had goodness and light in him at one time in his life but had given over to the Dark Side, from which there was no apparent return. My only hope was to keep faking it, so that others wouldn't ever know the truth about me … and most important, so I wouldn't have to face it myself.

∾

Many times in my life, I have felt like the Steppenwolf in Herman Hesse's novel of the same name. The main character describes himself as a "Steppenwolf" because he feels torn between two natures inside himself, which are often opposing each other. The Steppenwolf is described as:

A wolf of the Steppes that had lost its way and strayed into the towns and the life of the herd, a more striking image could not be found for his shy loneliness, his savagery, his restlessness, his homesickness, and his homelessness! . . . He went on two legs, wore clothes and was a human being but nevertheless he was in reality a wolf of the Steppes. He had learned a good deal of all that people of a good intelligence can, and was a fairly clever fellow. What he had not learned, however, was this: To find contentment in himself and his own life . . .

He finds in himself a human being, that is to say, a world of thoughts and feelings, of culture and tamed or sublimated nature, and besides this he finds within himself also a wolf, that is to say, a dark world of instinct, of savagery and cruelty, of unsublimated or raw nature! . . . In reality, however, every person, so far from being a unity, is in the highest degree a manifold world, a constellated heaven, a chaos of forms, of states and stages, of inheritances and potentialities.

Like the Steppenwolf, I too have felt like there were at least two conflicting forces within me, "a chaos of forms, of states and stages," that are in a constant struggle of war and peace within my own soul. There was a part of me that really wanted to be a respected member of the "towns" and "of the herd," but another part felt almost driven to be the rebel so I could run away as far as possible from the superfluous demands of others. Thus the street kid called me back to the failure and self-destruction necessary to feed my addiction of running back to the streets where I really belonged.

The classes and training in my college studies encouraged self-reflection. The subjects called for a higher learning and a better understanding of how personalities were shaped and formed. Many professors tried to teach me how to help others with new techniques of getting underneath the presenting problems, to the source of their internal conflict. I "learned" how to get others in touch with their pain and how to help them find a "better" place to live their lives in harmony with themselves. *I just didn't learn how to make it work in my life.*

I had learned how to be successful in school. That had become almost easy compared to being successful in life. Not that I hadn't gotten better at making it *look* like I was successful ... but I knew the truth.

I was still hiding. I was hiding from others. I was hiding from myself. And I was hiding from life.

∽

3

"THE GOOD LIFE"

Oh the good life, full of fun seems to be the ideal
Mm, the good life lets you hide all the sadness you feel
Sung by Tony Bennett

I hadn't always felt the need to hide from life. I remember feeling loved and secure in our family home many times.

I was born in St. Paul, Nebraska, which was the childhood home of both of my biological parents. My first actual childhood memories, however, are of Kirkwood, Missouri, where we lived most of the first six years of my life.

I love the thoughts of those years. My memories of Kirkwood are of warmth and security and special love, and yet, as I reflect upon those days, I suddenly realize that I can hardly remember my father there.

My dad was a band director at a local high school, and I have an awareness of feeling proud of him—I was always proud of him—but I don't remember him simply being *there* in my world. The only actual memory I have of him during that time is of watching him perform at a football game. I was with my mother and older sister in the grandstand. It was halftime, and the marching band, with my dad as director, began to perform. Some high school kids near us started ridiculing the way my dad was marching.

My mother turned to them and admonished them,
saying, "That's these children's father you're talking about."
I felt anger and defensiveness. How dare they talk about my
dad like that. Didn't they know who he was? He was *my* dad.
I was so proud of him, and I wanted to be so much like him.
And yet, looking back, I'm not even sure I knew who he was.
I don't even remember him spending any time with me.

I do have memories of times as a family together. In the
evening, we would often get in the car, go for an ice cream
cone, and as we drove along, sing together. I remember songs
such as "Down by the Old Mill Stream" during which we
would echo the melody and harmonize together. Those times
formed for me a feeling of family unity during my first six
years, which, despite the lack of personal interaction with my
dad, has served as a basis for emotional stability in believing
that my early years were mostly characterized by relationships
based on love.

At the end of my first grade in school, we moved to a
small town outside of Rochester, New York, so that my dad
could complete his Ph.D. in music at the Eastman School
of Music. We rented an old farmhouse in Parma Corners,
New York, and I started the second grade in a two-room
schoolhouse with grades one through three in one room,
and four through six in the other. I was the only boy in the
second grade with seven girls, and I remember being the
center of much attention. I also remember not minding that
at all.

My mom and dad worked at odd jobs—nights in a drive-in theater selling concessions, etc.—to supplement Dad's education funds. My mother had a specialty that produced both income and acclaim. She crafted handmade puppets out of papier-mâché and sold them in various places.

A Spanish family stopped by one day, having seen the sign by our house, which read "Puppets for Sale." After politely touring the basement of our house, viewing the puppet-making process, the man suddenly asked my mom, "But, where are the puppas?" My mother replied, "These *are* the puppets."

Then with a remorse that I still feel in his voice, he explained that all he wanted was a puppy for his children. He thought we had dogs for sale. I am still aware of my sensitivity to his hurt and embarrassment.

My New York memories center on the two-room school, my "girl-friends," and my mother's puppets. I remember hearing my dad practicing his trombone but little else, with one very notable exception.

The only interaction that I recall between my dad and me is a time when he was walking in front of me about ten yards or so. I had a penny in my hand and, for reasons unknown, threw it as hard as possible at my dad's head, never dreaming it would hit the target. It certainly did, however, and his response made a lasting impression upon my mind, to say nothing of the indentation of his hand upon my butt.

At the end of that year in New York, we moved to
Arkansas. Dad had taken a position at Ouachita College in
Arkadelphia. Life there has always represented happiness
to me.

Our family consisted of Mom and Dad, me, and two
sisters, Kathie, who was five years older, and Libby, who was
five years younger, than me. My parents purchased a beautiful
home in a nice neighborhood, and right from the beginning,
I had most things that kids wanted at that age. I had lots
of friends, became involved in a Cub Scout group (for
which my mom was the den mother), and enjoyed the many
activities of our church and school. My dad was a respected
member of the community, and the feelings of security and
pride that I had about him and our whole family contributed
to a sense of love and well-being that made everything seem
so beautiful and complete.

My dad never interacted with me, that I remember, in
playing catch or fishing, but I was so proud of him as a
college professor that I really began to idolize him.

Just before my fifth-grade year, we moved to Missoula,
Montana. Dad had been offered a better position with
a larger university, and with regret on my part in leaving
Arkadelphia, we made the transition. Even though the
following year is hazy in my mind, it seems as though things
were fine. I became involved in school and activities with
friends, and best of all, began to play the trombone. People
commented on my natural talent, comparing my ability to

my dad's, and that pushed me even harder to excel. There was no doubt in my mind that when I grew up I would be a music professor and maybe even an entertainer, for my dad had played in bands and orchestras, and I was going to be just like him!

Then one day, toward the end of the year, I came home from school to find my mother sobbing uncontrollably on the living room floor. She was holding a letter from a man who said that my dad was running around with his ex-wife and that the affair had been going on for quite a while. This woman was a grade school music teacher—my music teacher at school. My dad later admitted the affair and wound up moving out of our house, asking my mother for a divorce.

My whole world came crashing down around me. The stability of our home and everything I was and ever wanted to be were wrapped up in my dad, and now he was gone. How could it be possible that our happy, stable family could be so devastated by my fine, respected father?

Much later in my adult life, the truth finally came out. Dad had always been "running around" with women. It had happened many times before, since long before my birth; it even happened in Arkansas. Mother had always gotten him to come back, thus our family had been maintained as "happy" and "respected," but this was the end.

In the months to follow, Dad pursued the divorce and even told my mother that he wanted nothing to do with her or her kids. I felt completely lost and abandoned by the major person in my life.

My mother and my two sisters and I moved from Missoula that summer to the little town of Sunnyside, Washington, where Mom got a job as a speech therapist, traveling from school to school in neighboring towns. I was in the sixth grade and was able to make friends and still played the trombone in school. Things were all right, but I began to wet the bed every night.

A couple of times that first year after the divorce, I ran away from home, thinking that I should try to get back to Arkansas, because I had so many friends there and everything would be happy again. One of those times, I was hitchhiking on a lonely country road near Pendleton, Oregon, when a policeman stopped. He asked me how old I was. Being only eleven, I lied and said I was sixteen, thinking he'd let me go on my way.

Next he asked where I was headed, and I said, "Arkansas." He asked why I was going there, and the only thing I could think of to say was, "If I can get back to Arkansas, everything will be happy again. I just gotta get back to Arkansas."

The officer took me to headquarters, put me in a little cell, and after making me tell the truth, he told me to remember what jail was like, because that was where I'd end up if I kept lying and running away. He called my mom, and she came to pick me up.

My life back in Arkansas became the fantasy that I
formulated in my troubled mind: Arkadelphia, Arkansas, was
where everybody got along together, where all the elements
of the "good life" were experienced. As far as I knew, there
was no poverty or hardships, and everybody in town had
good jobs, had nice houses to live in, got along well with
their neighbors, had well-behaved kids ... and most of
all, had great family relationships, with lots of love. It was
the place where we should have stayed as a family. If we
had stayed, none of the chaos and heartbreak would have
happened.

I reasoned that someday I would get back there. I would
live with any number of families who would want me. I made
the decision to do anything I could to go back and started
running away.

❧

«I think that may be the point where you
started getting off track.»

"Ya think so?"

〜

Later that year, my mother met the man whose wife my dad
had run away with, and their loneliness and the situation
drew them together. Within a few months, my mother

remarried—to the man whose ex-wife my dad was now married to.

We moved to Seattle, where my new stepfather got a job as a food chemist. We had a beautiful home on the lake, but we were not a family. My older sister had gotten married the year before at age sixteen, and my six-year-old sister seemed to adapt easily. However, I did not fit into the new structure.

It was at this point in my life that I began to hide. I certainly didn't tell anyone that I wet the bed almost every night. It was embarrassing enough just being a kid who had only one parent and not enough money to have new clothes or a nice house in a good neighborhood. I also didn't know how to explain the situation with my parents. When I tried to tell people, they would usually laugh and exclaim, "Your parents switched partners!"

"No way," I tried to say at first. "It wasn't like they all went out together on a date and decided that they each liked the other partner better." But it just became easier to not talk about it. It became easier to hide the truth from others, and it especially became easier to hide the feelings from myself.

∾

4

"MY WAY"

For what is a man, what has he got?
If not himself, then he has naught.
To say the things he truly feels:
And not the words of one who kneels.
The record shows I took the blows—
And did it my way!
                    Sung by Frank Sinatra

I am thankful for the early beginnings in my life, and even though my world and my hope for the future were almost completely destroyed by the events that transpired after my parents' divorce, the beginnings provided a solid foundation upon which I could later build in parenting my own children.

I knew that I didn't want to treat my children the way I'd been treated, yet not having a role model to follow, I had to make up my parenting style by what "felt" right.

I remember an incident with Eric, one of my four children, when he was five years old. He came running in for dinner one Saturday evening about six o'clock and said, "Can I go back to Michael's after dinner?" Without thinking, I answered, "No." He asked, "Why not?" I told him, "Because you've been over there all day." He seemed to accept that and asked what we were going to do together after dinner.

I replied, "Nothing, because I have to study," being a full-time doctoral student at the time. He said, "Okay, Dad. What's Mom going to do with us after dinner?" I replied, "Your mom has a headache and won't even be joining us for dinner." Eric seemed to ponder this for a moment, with his bright eyes darting back and forth.

Eric then repeated my words with a quizzical tone to his voice. "Okay, so you can't do anything with us after dinner because you have to study, and Mom has a headache and won't even be joining us for dinner ..." Then after a long pause during which he seemed to be weighing the "logic" in my answers, he asked, "So why can't I go to Michael's after dinner?" I was immediately tempted to repeat the phrase that I had heard so often from authority figures, such as police, teachers, probation officers, detention staff, and others who would not allow their personal power to be questioned: "Because I said so!" But those words had always frustrated me, causing me to reflect on my own stupidity, feeling more discouraged than I had before.

It seems to me that when parents use that phrase, it's because they really don't know what else to say. Wanting to be good parents but not having the skills necessary to expand their answers, they just resort to giving the child a lesson in obeying authority, regardless of whether it makes any sense ... even to a five-year-old!

Was I really going to tell my son that I was the supreme authority on making nonsensical decisions, and then tell him to sit down, shut up, and watch TV for the rest of the evening?

The dreaded truth was that I didn't have a clue why he couldn't go to Michael's after dinner. All the training in the world can't prepare the parent for the answers to daily life questions when raising children. The question is not if we know the answer; the question is if we are going to admit to the child that we don't know.

Are we afraid that if we are honest with our children about our true lack of knowledge that it will cause them to doubt or disrespect everything we say or do from that point on? Does honesty breed disrespect? Absolutely not! It breeds just the opposite: *respect and trust*.

Thomas Szasz is quoted as saying: "Every act of conscious learning requires the willingness to suffer an injury to one's self-esteem. That is why young children, before they are aware of their own self-importance, learn so easily."

Even at that point in my life during which I was "faking it" with so many people, I refused to pass on to my children the feelings of humiliation and defeat that I experienced when I heard, "Because I said so!"

I responded to Eric, "I guess you're right. Of course you can go to Michael's after dinner."

I have personally found that one of the greatest ways to enhance self-esteem in children is to *apologize* when we have handled an intervention poorly and dumped our anger or frustration upon them. Another self-esteem builder is to be willing to try to see their viewpoint and *change our minds* when they make better sense than we do.

«Seems like you do a lot of apologizing. Why don't you just learn to quit making so many mistakes instead?»

"Sorry, some things take a while to learn."

I am not saying that parents must always give permission to their children or that the child's logic is always superior to that of the adult, but when that is so obviously the case, being open and honest with our children will not create disrespect for our leadership. In fact, the opposite is true, as they respect and honor us for the willingness to change our viewpoints and ideas. Thus we begin the process of helping our children increase their own feelings of *SELF-ESTEEM.*

I can't put enough emphasis on the value of a loving, solid beginning for the life of a child. I've spent a lot of hours working as a therapist with children and teenagers who didn't have the advantages that I did in my early years. Many of those kids just didn't have the opportunity to bond or make a lasting connection with the caregivers in their lives. There are a lot of underlying reasons for the lack of bonding,

beyond the scope of this book, but one of the primary issues
centers on the lack of opportunity to develop trust.

It may seem that trust can be shattered at any age, but
for the child in the first few years of life, trust is essential
for further development throughout the life cycle. The lack
of a solid connection with caregivers is often because the
needs of the parents outweigh the needs of the child. This
may happen because of addictions, trauma, disruptions in
relationships, or anything that drives the caregiver toward
the object of his or her own desire with such a force that
it overrides the natural instinct to provide the consistent
parenting the child must have.

In these cases, a parent may lavish attention upon the
child one day (often driven by guilt) and completely ignore
him or her the next day. The child doesn't know *when* or *if*
his or her desires will be satisfied and therefore cannot trust
anything or anyone. Therapy with kids who are un-bonded
from an early age is difficult at best and requires a lot of
caring and consistency.

Trust is one of the primary elements in the development
of self-esteem. Children not only need to know their needs
will be met consistently but also, as they grow older, that
their feelings and ideas have meaning to others. A lot of
people refer back to someone special, such as a teacher,
doctor, or pastor, who helped change the course of their
thinking and the direction of their lives. I believe that
whatever these people did to connect emotionally, it inspired

others to start believing in themselves—to believe that there was something of value in them, no matter what the circumstances.

One of the people who did that for me was Bob Schmidt. Bob was a probation officer at the Juvenile Detention Center in Medford, Oregon. I don't know how he did it, but he made me believe that I could actually do something positive with my life.

Bob felt differently than the probation officer who came to my dad's house and told him that I would spend the rest of my life behind bars. Bob's belief in me planted the idea that if I ever got my life together I would like to be a counselor like Bob.

Of course many other people have had a positive influence on me, but most of their influence was overshadowed by my own negative self-image, thus I didn't realize their impact on me until much later in life.

The following concepts are presented both as an overall *goal* for parents and caregivers to help instill in all children and also as an easily remembered *guide* for use during any specific discipline situation. I offer two things to parents and caregivers as goals for children when the opportunity presents itself in teaching or counseling. They are easy to remember but much harder to accomplish. I believe parents need to give each child many opportunities to develop:

SELF-ESTEEM and SELF-CONTROL.

To enhance *self-esteem* during a specific interaction with
a child (especially when we are frustrated with his attitude
and/or behavior), we should ask ourselves, "Are my words
or my actions *at this moment* going to increase the child's
self-esteem or make him feel worse about himself?" As
we attempt to focus on the negative behavior so the child
can learn from his mistakes, we need to be certain that our
interventions do not further discourage the child. If a child
can feel *good about himself* and also have the opportunity to
choose his own behavior as often as possible, that child is
much more likely to make *healthy choices* that will continue for
a lifetime.

Self-control is the other goal that I strongly advocate. Over
the years, I have worked with many parents who wish to
control their children by giving them permission for activities
and choices only once the parents have fully investigated
the negative potential of their children's request. It is not so
much that they want to "control" them, but to "protect"
them. The problem occurs when that protection begins to
incapacitate their children, leaving them with little ability to
protect themselves or to choose the path that is best suited for
them—or give them the opportunity to develop self-control.

When my son Brian was in the seventh grade, he came
into my room and burst into tears. He said, "Dad, I'm
having problems ... I'm smoking marijuana."

I have used this example many times in parenting classes
and in counseling well-meaning but frustrated parents by

asking them how they might handle a similar statement from their son. Some of the answers were as follows: "I would ask where he got it"; "I want to know which friends of his are involved, so I can keep him from being with them"; "I would ground him for two weeks so he would break the addictive pattern." Some parents have even said, "I would search his room or call the police. We have to nip this in the bud."

My first response to these parents was to say, "But he is voluntarily bringing this information to me, and if I punish him for his truthfulness, he simply won't bring any more of his problems to me. We don't even train our pet dogs this way. If we punish them after calling them, they will avoid us as much as possible. Shouldn't we treat our children at least as well as our pets?"

With Brian, I asked him to sit down with me and tell me what was bothering him. He told me that he felt a lot of peer pressure to smoke it but didn't really like the effects. We talked for a half-hour or so about choices and how hard it was to know which way to go sometimes, especially when there were feelings of conflict. At the end of our discussion, I told him to let me know what decision he made about it and that I would support his choice. About three days later, he told me that he had decided to quit and thanked me for talking to him about it.

But would I have *really* supported his choice if he had decided to continue smoking? Of course I would have, because it is not so much the decision that I believe in but Brian himself. I want him to make good choices when he is alone, without my consultation, but I know that cannot happen if he has not learned from his own failures along the way.

I could have deluded myself into thinking that Brian would quit simply because I forbade it. But I knew better. The best thing I could do for Brian was to keep the line of communication open so he could trust that I would always be approachable.

The entire incident served primarily to enhance the TRUST in our relationship, so that Brian would know that he could talk to me about anything, no matter how large or small it was to him.

∽

There are many choices our children will face that require our intervention, lest our children be placed needlessly in harm's way. But to constantly choose for them just because we know the potential pitfalls is to keep them ill-equipped to deal effectively with the pitfalls that life may bring anyway.

I have often counseled parents who keep a vigil over their teenagers' sleepovers, activities with friends, overnight trips, or a host of similar situations in which the potential for harm may exist. But more often than not, the harm is realized because of the youths' poor choices when the parents could not have been present to help in any case. Especially as our children grow older, into their teenage years, we have to allow them to experience life with both the good and the bad consequences, with fewer and fewer interventions on our part.

I am often asked at what age I recommend allowing youths to make some of these decisions without parental involvement. It is certainly true that the appropriate age will vary with the situation and the child, but the underlying principle of allowing children to know that their opinions and ideas are important in making decisions will work at any age.

As soon as possible, the parent must cultivate a relationship with the child that includes vulnerability and openness, so both of them *trust* that they can be heard by the other, without rejection.

We often hear from parents, "As soon as you're eighteen and out of high school, you can do what you want." However, if youths have not been able to choose some of what they want before that time, they may well explode onto the scene of personal "freedom" with a bang that will hurt for a long time to come.

Self-esteem and self-control are two qualities that parents should encourage as they guide their children toward reaching their own potential. Without these qualities, children and teenagers may find themselves in situations that destroy their whole world ... as happened to me when my self-esteem and self-control were shattered that terrible day after we moved to Seattle.

❦

5

"RUNAWAY"

I'm a-walkin' in the rain,
Tears are fallin' and I feel the pain,
Wishin' you were here by me,
To end this misery
>> Sung by Del Shannon

I will never forget the first time that my new stepfather
hit me. We were in the car. He was in the driver's seat, my
mother and little sister in the back seat, and I was in the
front seat. We had just pulled up to our new house, which
was one block up the hill from Lake Washington, with a
beautiful view looking eastward across the lake. It seemed so
peaceful, a great place to start our new life.

I am not sure what was happening in the car, but I think
I was arguing with my mother about something. Suddenly,
he backhanded me on the right side of my face with such
force that my head slammed backward into the door frame. I
saw the horrified looks of my mother and sister. I think my
mother began to protest, but I don't remember anything that
was actually said.

I had never been hit by an adult in the face, or even hit
that hard by anyone or anything.

I was tall for my age and had banged my head into a lot of things in the past. I had gotten into a couple of fights in school before. But nothing compared to this blow, which came out of nowhere, with no warning or anticipation.

Although that moment is frozen in my mind, I remember nothing of the events immediately before or after it happened. I don't even remember much about the year following that experience.

I was a seventh grader at Jane Addams Junior High School. The school had over 1500 kids, but I didn't make any friends that I hung out with. I didn't have anybody come to our house or anybody to stay overnight.

I was still pretty good on the trombone and played in the band. I was even the leader of the trombone section and sat in the honored position of "first chair," until one day when I lost a challenge for the placement. Within a few days, I had fallen all the way to "last chair."

I felt like my life was at the bottom, and that was fine with me because down there, nobody paid much attention to or had many expectations of me.

I don't remember any interaction or activities at home, or doing anything with the "family." My maternal grandmother came to live with us for a while, and died that year. I don't know how long she stayed with us before she died. I can't even remember her there.

I also don't remember my stepfather hitting me again. Many years later, when I was seeing a therapist for my problems as an adult, my mom told my therapist during a session that she had moved out and separated from my stepfather because she came home from work one day and found her husband standing over me as I lay on the dining room floor. She told my therapist that she saw him kick me in the head area and knew she needed to leave with her children. She was surprised that I couldn't remember it happening. Later I told my therapist that I had pictured that scene many times but as if I was watching it from across the room. I always thought it was just a bad dream.

Evidently there were other times, but he had promised to stop. I always knew that my mom had left my stepfather because of me, but I had thought it was because of all the things that I did and the trouble that I got into; I thought it was my fault.

Children often blame themselves for the chaos in the family. I was no exception. I felt that I was a failure in everything because my life was in shambles around me. My only hope was to run away from it all.

I don't remember much about home or school, but I remember a lot about my experiences on the streets. I ran away as often as I could manage it.

At first, I would skip school and wander around the area in which we lived, called Lake City. Soon, however, I made my way to downtown Seattle and was gone overnight or for days at a time. I enjoyed the nighttime activity down by Pioneer Square, on skid row, where winos and vagrants and homeless people lived.

For many years afterward, I felt like I was always thirteen as I reflected back on the lessons learned from the street kid. In fact, it seems like the street kid in me is perpetually thirteen, as I still feel the constant struggle of early adolescence— wanting to be independent, feeling awkward about my mind and my body, and wondering what to do with my life.

❧

«Well, you may not like being thirteen, but I like it ... as long as I can lie about being older when I need to.»

"Don't you think that it would be good to grow up someday?"

«Sure ... good for you. That will make you seem more like a real doctor.»

෴

I don't know how many times I actually ran away, how often I was without a safe place to sleep, why I was even there at all—it all just seems jumbled up in my mind and stuck there in my thirteen-year-old self.

I began to learn the ways of the streets, and it was there that I felt most at home. I remember seeing skinny old men in sleeveless T-shirts leaning out of the windows of old hotels. They seemed to be always smoking cigarettes as they stared blankly at the life on the street. I always thought (and still do sometimes) that when I was old I would wind up there. The thought scared me at times but also offered relief—I would have a regular place to stay, with no responsibilities, no family, and no problems.

I was twelve to thirteen but around six foot three, and when I covered my thin boyish frame with a motorcycle jacket, jeans, biker boots, and sunglasses, I could pass for a young adult. I got into certain bars, which I then frequented and became known as one of the regulars. Bartenders didn't ask for I.D. because most of the street people didn't have identification anyway. The police were usually too busy with people who were causing problems to notice me, and I tried to stay as far out of sight as possible, though there were a few notable exceptions.

One of the places that I hung out in was called the Britannia, which was on the corner of First Avenue across from Pioneer Square. One afternoon, a fortyish, short, stocky Hispanic man in a long topcoat announced loudly that "we" had been insulted by the patrons of the White Rock tavern, around the corner on Occidental. He stated that "they" (who were mostly of African-American descent) had made racial slurs about us (who were mostly Hispanic and Native American, except for one white teenager who tried to hide who he was and where he was from).

Our "champion" asked for a group of volunteers to fight them on a prearranged corner across the street.

I, of course, jumped up, hoping to blend into the crowd and to show willingness to fight for our honor.

Following him across the street, I looked back and was very dismayed that no one else was with us. I couldn't let him see that I was just a scared kid, so I continued on. When we got to the corner, he handed me a baseball bat that he had hidden and took out his knife. At that moment, a group of several guys from the White Rock came walking around the corner heading directly towards us.

To this day, I don't know why the next few moments happened the way they did. My leader jumped in front of me into the middle of the street and started slashing the air with his knife. I stayed a few steps behind him, holding my bat up. As the group of five or six guys approached, they all stared wide-eyed at us, paused briefly, and then turned and ran back around the corner. I don't know if they were just terrified by the realization that two crazy people would stand up against a larger group, or as I've often thought, God placed a host of angels behind us because he didn't want us to be slaughtered.

Whatever the reason, it worked, and we walked back across First Avenue into the Britannia. My new best friend kept telling people that I was the "only one" who was brave enough to stand up with him for our cause.

We were *heroes!* Everybody chipped in to buy us several rounds of beer. Shortly after that, a policeman came in to ask if anyone knew anything about the incident, but nobody told him who we were.

There were other times when my survival seemed to defy explanation. As my mother, Venus Bardanouve, wrote in her own book entitled *Journeys of the Heart*:

> I am still awed when I recall how God protected us, especially my twelve-year-old son, Ric, who was greatly troubled by the loss of his father. I was desperately searching for ways to help him adjust to the upheaval in our lives.
>
> One Sunday, I saw an advertisement of a mountain cabin for rent and thought, "Perhaps a boy would find interesting and happy things to do on weekends in that setting." The cabin was listed with a realtor in a small town forty miles from our city. My young daughter and I drove to the town, without my realizing that the idea to go there was surely God-inspired.
>
> As I drove into town and braked at a stop sign, I was stunned to see Ric on the street corner. I knew he had been upset when he left our home that afternoon, but I just thought he was somewhere in the neighborhood. He was relieved to see us, and, as he climbed into our little Volkswagen, told me he had decided to run away—where, he did not know. He had hitched a ride, and the driver had left him in that town.
>
> How could I have driven all those miles through the city to the very place he stood! Only God could have

watched over him and directed me to that spot to bring
home a frightened and confused boy.

I remember seeing my mom and sister drive up to the corner. At first, I was disappointed because I had been caught, but then I felt safe and secure again ... until the next time something triggered my growing addiction to running away.

∽

To survive on the streets, I *faked* being a bad, tough guy—nobody to mess with, somebody to be left alone. I remember standing on the corner of Main and Occidental one afternoon, when a carload of guys pulled up next to me and stopped.

A black guy stuck his head out of the back window and menacingly said, "Hey, boy. Do you want to get in this car before somebody do something to you?"

With as much vehemence in my voice as I could muster, I snapped back, "Hey, boy. Do you want to move on before somebody do something to *you*?"

The car moved on slowly as I glared at them, waiting for them to make any sudden moves. As soon as they drove around the corner, I walked toward First Avenue where there were more people standing around together.

Inside I was trembling. *Oh, brother! If I had gotten in that car I would have been kidnapped, tortured, and murdered! I better think about getting something to defend myself with if necessary.*

I also learned how to survive by lying. It was called *hustling*, and I hustled every person and in every way that I could. During business hours, I would hustle people on the street uptown by telling them hard-luck stories and even gaining sympathy by convincing people of my real age. I started learning how to play pool, and even though I wasn't very good at it, I used it to hang out with people who had money.

There were some poolrooms in downtown Seattle that stayed open late into the night, and there, I could watch and learn, and at least stay out of the rain. They offered a safe, warm place where there were people to connect with. Older men would sometimes offer instruction in playing the game or in poolroom etiquette or in learning how to "read" people and their intentions, so you know who to connect with and who to stay away from.

I also met a lot of hustlers—not just pool players, but people who made their living trying to make a fast, easy buck without doing any "work." The small-time hustlers would try to draw you into their latest scheme, which was doomed to fail, because the hustler stood out with an approach that screamed, "I'm a two-bit con artist that is ready to take you for all your chump-change, because I can't figure out how to hustle you for any big money!" There were others though who personalized being "cool." They would only play for serious money, were usually really good at the game, but were also interested in many other aspects of life in general. These "teachers" taught me that pool is mostly a mental game.

"You have to see the shot in your mind. You have to visualize the point on the object ball where you want the cue ball to hit. You see the place on the table where you want the cue ball to stop for position on the next shot. You imagine the object ball on a direct line straight into the center of the pocket. Then you bend down and execute it just like you saw it in your mind—just like everything else in your life that you *really* want, you've got to *see* it, and then make it happen."

Pool players talk about "getting in stroke." They learn to lock everything out of their minds for the moment and visualize every shot on the table, *knowing* that the balls are going in the pockets ... because they are in stroke.

David McCumber describes it so well in his book *Playing Off the Rail*:

> *That wondrous mental realm of awareness and acuity that pool players call "dead stroke," "dead punch," having the cue ball on a "string," in a "trance"...*
>
> *There is that attainable but ephemeral "zone," born of confidence, competence, concentration, and the positive focusing of emotion and spirit, that produces spectacular results. It is the essence of success, the Holy Grail of sports psychologists. In some measures, it is what we all seek in our lives. Dead Stroke.*

I also learned how to relate to others in many walks of life, and a lot of the wisdom that came from my experiences on the streets had its birth in the poolrooms of Seattle.

I remember thinking, I *love poolrooms. I love going to the Paris ... what's the full name? Ben Paris Sporting and Recreation, something like that. Some people are starting to nod to me when I come in. I nod my head back to them. I feel good there. There's always something happening ... pool action for money. I like to watch and listen and learn.*

In pool halls, I did learn. I learned that I probably would never be one of the great pool players. My mind always betrayed me by thinking too much about other things when I needed to stay focused on the shot or the strategy for the moment.

But while I wasn't going to be great (or even really good) in playing pool, it was different when it came to people. I seemed to be more gifted in "public relations." It became one of the most important elements of my "game"—to get along with others, avoid fights, gain other people's trust ... and blend in as much as possible.

My game was all about getting money—money to eat or get a hotel room or even get into the all-night theater on First Avenue.

Just down First Avenue across the street from the Pennyland Arcade (where I spent a lot of time) was the Rivioli Theatre. People on the street called it the "all-night theater" because the movies would run until six in the morning. I have no idea what movies they played because, like most of the patrons, I went there to sleep when the weather was cold or rainy and I didn't have enough money to get a room somewhere.

As long as you paid the admission price and didn't leave, you could stay inside all night. I always wore sunglasses and pulled a wool cap down to my eyes, so as to hide most of my boyish features that might give me away or make me look vulnerable.

One night after I first started going there, a guy in the same row a couple of seats down from me leaned over and whispered, "Be careful in here ... you never know when somebody might try to grab or hurt you, so sleep with one eye open."

Not knowing or trusting his real intentions, I grunted back, "They will be in for a big surprise if that happens, because I am a judo master and their heads will bounce all over the back of these theater seats as they go down."

Fortunately, I never had to demonstrate these well-honed fantasy skills. It wasn't long before I became sort of a *regular* there, and people left me alone.

There were many times when I had to use my "tough guy" facade to keep predators from getting too close. If any of them had seen what I really was, I'd have been a victim of the night and the streets in a heartbeat.

∽

I met a lady one time while she was huddled in a doorway to get out of the rain. She was much older than I was, in her late thirties or forties, but she seemed somewhat attractive to me. We started talking, and I found out that she had all her possessions in a paper sack and no place to stay. As we talked, I suggested that we might try to get enough money to get a room together. She thought I meant that we would have a sexual experience and said to me, "You don't even know if you'd like to kiss me."

I was actually terrified, having never kissed anyone before. But not wanting to reveal anything about my true identity, I told her that we would "find that out when we get to the room." I was a thirteen-year-old boy imprisoned in a man's body, but although my body may have looked like an adult's, my mind was always in conflict. No matter how hard I tried to forget my age, I often felt caught between the kid I was and the adult I was pretending to be.

It was at that point that I knew I couldn't spend the night with her, but I was still determined to find someone or some way to help her get a place. Shortly afterwards, I found a guy that I had seen before and asked him to help, introducing us as "mother and son." He took us to the Kenneth Hotel on First Avenue and Cherry Street, where he got us a room. I told her it didn't seem right to sleep together since I had made the "mistake" of introducing us as mother and son. I told her that I would find another place to stay and would come get her in the morning.

When I came back from the all-night theater in the morning, I went directly to her room at the hotel. Her door was open, and a stranger was searching through her bag. I noticed some blood drops on the bag, and in the toughest voice that I could muster, I demanded to know what had happened. He replied that the woman had cut her wrists and had been taken to the hospital.

Terrified and bewildered, I ran out into the street, and even though I didn't know much about prayer, I prayed God would save her life and keep her safe. I never found out.

That was one of the times that I went back to my mother and stepfather's house in North Seattle. Of course I could have gone back anytime, and sometimes did, but the streets were becoming the place where I felt more at home. With my newly found adult role as a "street-wise tough guy," I may have actually been safer on the streets than at home with my stepfather.

❧

6

"GOTTA SERVE SOMEBODY"

> You're gonna have to serve somebody, yes indeed
> You're gonna have to serve somebody.
> Well, it may be the devil or it may be the Lord
> But you're gonna have to serve somebody.
>   Sung by Bob Dylan

Doyle, the epitome of a horrible stepfather, in the movie *Sling Blade* rekindles my feelings about my own stepfather every time I hear him say:

> *See, here's the deal, Frank. If I'm going to throw my life away doing what I want to come live with y'all, we're gonna get some shit straight. See, your mom and I don't have no problems except for you. Fact is, we don't have a bad word between us. But since you do exist and I'm gonna be the head of the household, you're gonna learn to live by my rules, and the first rule is: you don't speak unless you are spoken to. You got me? And you stay the hell out of my way, and do what a regular kid does. You're a weird little shit, Frank, and I don't get you. So wake up and face what they call reality. See, we're gonna be a family, Frank ... my family ... I'll be paying all the bills. That means you're stuck with my ass. But I ain't your daddy; you just act like I am!*

The unbelievable "reality" and cruelty of that message is that it most likely typifies the attitude and parenting style of more parents and stepparents than we would ever dare to believe.

I certainly don't remember my stepfather sitting me down and talking to me about his rules or his family, or about anything else for that matter. However, when I hear that "sermon" in the movie or find out about a parent who displays that kind of treatment toward a child, the anger that I feel from deep inside brings the realization of my own experience, even though I couldn't face it or allow awareness of it back then.

❧

"To tell you the truth, I think *bad thoughts* when any kid is treated that way."

"Me, too."

"On that point, I'm glad we think alike."

"Yeah!"

∽

In my role as a therapist and college teacher, I have worked with and taught many persons who are in troubled relationships with their children. As I have discovered in my own role as a parent, the trouble usually doesn't come from a lack of desire to be a *loving* parent; the trouble comes from a lack of knowledge about what to do to be a *good* parent.

The truth that most often presents itself in these situations is that, without training to do otherwise, we *parent as we were parented.* In my work, I have come across many parents who present such concepts as: "My dad used to take me out behind the woodshed and beat the tar out of me, and I used to hate it, but now I can see that I needed it, so that's why I do it now for my kids." The same applies to yelling, put-downs, smothering with control and rules, etc., in which the parents become the police, judge, jury, and jailer for their children, all in the name of love, passed down from generation to generation.

I have often thought that I was fortunate in not remembering the "love-beatings" I received. When it came to disciplining my own children, I didn't have a tradition to pass along. As a result, I at least tried to avoid that which didn't make any sense to me.

I just knew that I didn't want to be:

- Rejected
  - Ridiculed
    - Hit
      - Kicked
        - Yelled at
          - Overpowered

I did want to be:
- Listened to
  - Included
    - Respected
      - Appreciated
        - Valued

During the many times of uncertainty in parenting, I tried to remember what it *felt* like on the streets and treated my children as I had wanted to be treated before the abuse that drove me to run away.

That exercise led me to my first "rule" in parenting: always try to *listen* to what the child is saying or feeling, and try not to discourage him or her any further. My second "rule" followed: always try to *include* the child in the discussion of what permission should be given or what discipline should be involved.

Parents often ask what age their children should be to apply these "rules." My usual reply is the story of Eric at age five, which I relayed earlier. If I had not listened to his viewpoint, or if he had been fearful of my response, neither of us would have learned the lesson. Thus, I usually suggest that parents try it when their children are able to converse with them (verbally or non-verbally), so the parents can relate to what the child is feeling. There have been other "rules" that my experience and training have allowed me to

develop over the years, but the foundation of the first two
has given substance to the rest.

Of course I have failed many times to follow my own
standards.

In preparation for this book, Eric wrote about one of his
memories of my failures:

> *This is a memory of when I was a sophomore and
> living with you. That was a difficult time for both of us.
> I was really angry, failing school, and the most depressed
> that I have ever been.*
>
> *When you were there I felt that I had no
> relationship with you at all. Sometime within that
> period you had that huge crappy car that barely ran.
> Occasionally you would let me drive it by myself
> without a license. I had taken it to school one day and
> ran the left side right into a telephone pole. It was at a
> very low speed and the damage was not that noticeable. I
> was too frightened to tell you and I hoped you wouldn't
> notice, so I hid the fact.*
>
> *A few weeks later the car had problems and you
> took it to the guy you got it from, and apparently
> the internal damage was worse than the outside. You
> confronted me and I admitted to it.*
>
> *I pleaded that I had not hit it that hard.*
>
> *You yelled, "Well, how hard did you hit it? Did
> you hit it this hard?" as you slammed your hand on the*

> table. "Or did you hit it this hard?" and you kicked the
> table with all you had.
>
> I was terrified; I ran out the door and screamed
> that I was going to live at Jason's. To which you yelled
> back, "Fine, go live with Jason!"
>
> I recall this last comment really hurt because of
> the sincere tone of your voice. In my eyes it was the
> expression of rejection that I was feeling for months prior.
>
> I was most certainly wrong in the matter, and your
> anger may have been justified but could have manifested
> itself in a more productive way.

When Eric talks about being too frightened to tell me, it cuts to the bone. Because I hate being intimidated by others, I have struggled to watch my tone of voice and tried to ensure that others were not afraid of me. I obviously blew it a lot, and still do.

I have also failed with my other children as well. My oldest son, Clint, reminded me that in spite of my belief that there are many alternatives to hitting anyone, I used to apply the wooden spoon to his seat of knowledge on an all-too-regular basis. I think he is also glad that I had learned better by the time he was seven or eight. (Although I think that he may have wished I used it on his three younger siblings occasionally, in spite of the learning.)

My own self-image, my deep-seated anger, and my "street" persona as a manipulative, tough-guy hustler have served to derail my best intentions on numerous occasions, even with my own children. My "hiding" of my perceived "true identity" as an unintelligent, unlearned imposter in academic and social settings has often kept me from being sensitive and gentle with the needs of others who were searching for someone to listen and feel their pain.

I have most certainly failed ... but it is this failure that has driven my desire to change. In fact, it is my failures that have become my greatest asset in my search for wisdom that may offer direction to those who have lost their way.

William Saroyan gave insight to this possibility when he said, "Good people are good because they've come to wisdom through failure. We get very little wisdom from success you know."

∽

One of the underlying guidelines that I attempt to share with others about parenting is to utilize:

DISCIPLINE THAT PRODUCES DISCIPLES.

It seems to me that if parents could apply that concept to every intervention they invoke for the child's infractions, they would have much better success in helping the child learn from his or her mistakes.

Much "discipline" has very little instructive value in encouraging children to desire a change in their errant ways. In fact, in many cases, children are greatly motivated to change only one thing—getting caught—so they can avoid the harshness and punitive nature of the consequence.

No child wishes to receive discipline for his or her actions, but good, loving parents will always provide structure that helps the child learn not to repeat willful mistakes, in order to teach him or her to make better choices.

Scripture teaches that "God loves his children enough to discipline them." However, using the guideline of "discipline that produces disciples," it is difficult to imagine that Jesus would have encouraged many to follow him by using the angry, hurtful methods of some parents in today's culture. The dictionary defines *disciple* as a "follower of any teacher emphasizing learning." *Discipline* is defined (in part) as "training that develops self-control and character."

I try to envision Jesus yelling angrily at Peter, telling him that he had broken Jesus' trust, would be restricted from the boat for two weeks, and had better go to his room for a time-out period to think about it!

I have to say, that would not encourage much "discipleship" on my part. It might, however, create a feeling of fear of my "master," coupled with enough guilt to make me follow him around like a punished dog with my ears back and my tail between my legs.

When I have been faced with discipline situations with my own children, I asked myself, "Do I want them to fear me as the bad guy ... or follow me because they know that I believe in them for their own goodness?"

∽

One example with my oldest son, Clint, at the age of thirteen, illustrates these concepts. I was divorced from his mother, and Clint was living with just the two of us in the house. I had to go away for the weekend, and Clint elected to stay at home. I had a housekeeper named Debbie who stayed over with Clint when I was gone to provide meals and adult guidance when needed.

On Saturday, I called home to check on things, and Debbie told me a disturbing story of something that had happened the night before. "Someone tried to break into the house around midnight, and I called the police." Debbie went on to describe that she had been woken by the sound of the back door being rattled, so she grabbed her crowbar for protection and looked out the window.

She saw footprints in the snow and then heard the front door being shaken. After the police came, they followed the footprints in the snow, but they lost them down by the river. Debbie related that she was "terrified at the time" but was better now and reassured me that I didn't need to come home early.

I asked to speak to Clint, and he told me that he hadn't heard anything about it because he had spent the night at a friend's house.

When I returned home the next day, Clint met me at the door. The first thing he said to me was "Dad, I have something to tell you." He sighed and after a long pause said, "Well, you know that thing with Debbie on Friday night … that was me."

I responded incredulously, "You tried to break into your own house?" I could hardly keep from smirking as he said, "Well, there's a little more to it." I thought, *I bet there is. I can't wait to hear this one.*

Clint then explained that he had told Debbie he was going to stay with a friend, and the friend told his parents he was staying at Clint's. They had the night "free," and there was a party at a girl's house down the street from our house. The problem came when some high school boys showed up at the party, making it difficult for the eighth-grade boys to stay. Clint told his friend they could just sneak back into his house and make up some excuse to tell Debbie in the morning.

When they got to the house, they found that Debbie had locked the doors and windows (which wasn't our usual custom). He didn't ring the doorbell to wake her up because they had been drinking and didn't want to get caught. When they saw the police coming, they ran and later spent the night "freezing" in our unlocked van in the driveway.

After the sad telling of his tale, Clint said, "So what are you going to do about this, Dad?" Using my first two rules of *listening* and *including* the child in the discipline process, I asked Clint what he thought we should do. He stated that he knew it was serious but that he couldn't think of any consequence other than to "ground me for the rest of my life."

Clint knew I didn't believe grounding was usually helpful, because I wanted the consequence to have a more logical connection to the offense, but in this case, he couldn't think of any other option. I asked him if he would agree with anything that I decided, even if it was difficult for him to handle. He responded that he would do so.

My first intervention was the requirement of apologizing to Debbie for scaring her so badly that she was ready to kill the intruder with her crowbar. He quickly agreed and then said, "I didn't think about the crowbar" (knowing previously about Debbie's instrument to protect herself, kept under the bed). I was tempted to add insult to injury by remarking that "it is difficult to think clearly at all when you're out drinking," but I was getting the impression that Clint already knew that.

I also told him that because he had taken advantage of my being gone on a weekend, the next time that I had to go out of town for weekend business, he should remain at home, regardless if there was a game at school or a planned event that he was really looking forward to.

Then I told him that I would not call the other boy's parents and "rat" my son or his friend out, but I would not lie for him if they found out. I suggested Clint tell his friend that I knew about it and to head off disaster by telling them himself.

When the interaction was finished, I told Clint that I was *proud of him for telling me* and wanted to reward him by taking him out for a steak dinner at the restaurant of his choice.

Clint later told me that his friend was upset with him because he thought they had gotten away with it and wanted to know why Clint told me. Clint told him, "I trust my dad, and I don't lie to him." Clint said the other boy responded, "My dad will kill me if he finds out, and I hope he doesn't."

It's all about *discipline that produces disciples*.

I certainly didn't keep Clint from having his own failures, but even now as a young man in his late twenties, he has made a lot fewer than I have. Most important, my relationship with him is as free and open today as it has ever been.

I wanted that kind of relationship with my own father. Now I realize that his leaving our home upset me more because I *didn't* have a relationship with him ... and that was even harder to face in the glaring reality of an abusive stepfather. By the time my mother moved out of his house, I was addicted to the streets and my new role as an "adult"— and thus I was addicted to running away.

↬

7

"ON THE ROAD AGAIN"

On the road again—
Just can't wait to get on the road again.
Sung by Willie Nelson

I had just started my ninth-grade year in a new school in
Seattle. After school on the first day, I purposely missed
the bus, so I could hitchhike home to my mother's house in
Kenmore. Kenmore was a suburb just past the city limits of
Seattle near the north end of Lake Washington. My mother's
house was in a nice family neighborhood, but I had no
friends there.

I didn't want any friends there. The only "friends" I
had lived near Pioneer Square on skid row and the streets
downtown.

When a car stopped to pick me up, I opened the
passenger door and saw her. She was in her thirties and good
looking, and I could smell the booze. I threw my books into
the ditch by the side of the road, and when she asked me
what I had been carrying, I told her it was an old newspaper
with want ads for apartments. I wanted her to think I was an
adult looking for a new place to live. She offered to give me
a ride home, but I had her drive around for a while before I
finally told her that I didn't really want to go home.

She asked what I did want, and I told her that I'd like to go somewhere to drink some booze with her. She stopped at a small store, but the owner refused to sell anything to me. I went back out to the car and told her that I was only nineteen, so I couldn't buy any alcohol. She replied that she was thirty-five and could buy it for us. Then she took me to her apartment. We drank together and talked.

She told me that she was going through a divorce and that her husband was an attorney. She was afraid he would take her kids and leave her with nothing. She started to cry and said she was glad that I was there and that she wanted me to stay with her.

Then, in one of those moments that are frozen in my mind, she started to undress and asked if we should go in "the other room." I was excited and terrified at the same time. I replied, "You mean in the kitchen?" She responded, "No, silly, in the bedroom." She stood up, took my hand, and led me from the living room down the hallway to the bedroom.

I had never seen a woman naked before. I, of course, told her this was not my first time, but she had to show me everything to do. The rest of the night is blank in my mind. I had just turned fourteen and was in a state of shock, but like everything else in my life, I tried to hide it.

I stayed with her for a week. She stayed in bed most of the time and kept drinking. I spent most of my time learning to drive her car as I roamed all over Seattle. She lived in Mount Lake Terrace, which was near my mother's house in

Kenmore, so a couple of times I drove there to get some clothes, but my mother and sister were gone during the day, so I didn't get caught.

I don't remember much about the sexual experiences, but I slept with her every night.

∽

At the end of the week, I impulsively drove toward the highway leaving Seattle and headed south. I picked up a couple of hitchhikers who were both adult vagrants. I informed them that I was a judo master on a journey to Mexico but was short of cash for gas to make the trip. They both agreed that they would like to accompany me to Mexico, but neither of them had any money either.

It wouldn't be long before I discovered that they didn't believe my "judo master" identity, but they pretended to do so because I had the car. Of course, my "judo master" disguise was a ridiculous portrayal, but at my age, my mindset was formed by a childish attempt to keep myself "safe" on the streets. I just didn't realize how obvious my deception was.

When we arrived in Salem, Oregon, one of them suggested that we break into a gas station to search for money that may have been left from the day's business. While two of us waited in the car as lookouts, the other one pulled off the job. He returned with a couple of dollars in pennies and some "old coins" that he thought might be valuable to a coin collector.

We drove southward and pulled into the town of Albany, Oregon, in the dark of night, in the middle of a rainstorm, hoping for better success in our next "caper." Having only a week's worth of driving experience and with the poor visibility because of the rain, I ran a stop sign. The car behind me was a local policeman, who alerted me to his presence by turning on his top lights.

I told him my name was Richard Boyle (an alias I had often used on the street) and my age, which I said was twenty-two. Without a driver's license or any reasonable explanation for the car's ownership, I was taken, along with my traveling companions, to the city jail to await the police's further revelation about who we were and what our real purpose in Albany was.

The "old coins" did it. It turns out the coins were valuable enough for the station owner to describe them in a police report, which was put out on the law enforcement communication system.

The next day, the police told us the coins had been reported stolen, and one of my "crime partners," the one who waited in the car with me, told the whole story, no doubt trying to distance himself from the crime. The result was that we were all taken to the county jail in Salem, Oregon, to await trial.

Inside the jail, there was a long hallway with bars on both sides. On the left were two-man cells, and on the right was the day room (called the bull pen), where the men interacted with each other for most of the day.

My cellmate was a nice older guy, a preacher. He was in jail for "contributing to the delinquency of a minor," because he had allowed his seventeen-year-old to have a high school graduation party with a beer keg at his home. My cellmate told me that he didn't really believe in drinking but was convinced that his son and friends were going to drink anyway, and he would "rather see them in a house where they were safe and protected than being out somewhere else." He also stated that while he did not believe in drinking, he did believe in his son's ability to handle himself, and he still believed that he did the right thing in offering the party.

That preacher made a lasting impression on me, and I decided that if I ever became a father, I wanted to be like him. I knew that I wanted to have the kind of relationship with my children in which they knew that I would try to do the right thing for them even if the letter of the law said otherwise.

Salem, Oregon, is the site of the Oregon State Penitentiary, which meant the county jail was often full of adult men who were in for serious crimes. I remember one individual in his thirties who was being sentenced to life imprisonment for being a "habitual criminal," which meant that he had been so bad that the system was giving up on him. I, of course, wanted to hide my true identity, but my traveling companions blew my cover.

On the second day, they promptly told everybody that I was a "judo master" on a journey to Mexico. Several of the jailhouse leaders, including the new "lifer," pressed me to show them some of my moves.

I responded that my craft did not allow any display of technique, unless under specifically controlled conditions. They strongly suggested that the conditions in the jail met the criteria and I had better show my stuff.

The end result was my getting beaten up by a twenty-four-year-old criminal selected for that purpose. When they wanted to see if I could fare better with a lesser opponent, they picked a sixteen-year-old kid who was really so "tough and bad" that he was in the adult section of the county jail, to be tried as an adult for his crime. I wondered if his next crime might be the murder of a fourteen-year-old who was guilty of being a total fake.

I actually seemed to do better against him though and remember the fight being stopped when I punched his face and his head banged into the bars behind him. I had blood all over my white long-sleeved shirt, and a hole had been knocked through my lip, so I could squirt water out by closing my mouth and putting pressure on my lip from the inside.

I was given a nickname designed to humiliate me for my charade. They started calling me "Slimy Slim." "Slimy" because I represented myself as such a "bad, dirty street criminal" and "slim" because I was six foot six and weighed about 125 pounds.

Nobody talked to me much that day, and I sat in the corner of the bull pen feeling alone and humiliated.

❧

«I don't care. I like being alone; it's much safer.»

"But there's a time and place, and *that* wasn't it!"

«Enough said.»

❧

Late that afternoon, we went to court to hear the charges against us. The judge called our names and asked us to stand up. When he got to me, he asked if I was "Richard Boyle, age twenty-two."

I said, "No ... I'm Ric Cecil, and I'm fourteen years old." I was covered in blood, my white shirt ripped to shreds. The judge demanded that the county attorney inform him of the facts and asked, "Who is this boy, and what the hell is going on here?" The county attorney was visibly shaken as she stated that she didn't know but would find out. They took me to a side room, called my father at the college in Ashland, and confirmed my identity.

By the time the jailer took me back to get my personal belongings from my cell, the men had all heard the story. As

I passed by the bull pen on the way out with my things, the guys were all hooting and hollering about how "cool" I was and how well I had fought being only fourteen. As I got to the door to leave, I turned as if to say goodbye and flipped them off. Several of them lunged at me through the bars and pleaded with the jailer to let me back in for "just five seconds."

As I went down toward the juvenile section, I felt some satisfaction, but thought it might be wise to change the "judo master" part of my disguise in the future. Happily, I have never used it since. "Slimy Slim," however, would resurface in the not-too-distant future.

Much to my chagrin, I was placed back in the Juvenile Detention Center in Medford, Oregon, but I didn't know any of the kids.

Due to my previous escape attempt, they didn't let me out of my room very often. I had a lot of time to think about my life and all the changes that had occurred in the three previous very long years.

I decided that I had done pretty much all that I could ever want to do and had a "lifetime" of experience, and that now all of it was over. I didn't really think of killing myself, remembering my lady friend in the hotel, but I also knew I didn't want to live until I got into a similar situation.

I was taken before a juvenile court judge. My mother was on one side of the table and my father on the other. My mother had found a Christian Academy for troubled boys and asked the judge to place me there. The judge asked me what I wanted, with my choices being the academy or the McLaren State Reformatory in Woodburn. I replied, "I could care less what you do with me ... I have nothing left to live for."

A choice was made for me that no doubt impacted my identity in a powerful way. I was made a "ward of the court" of the State of Oregon and placed in the Vancouver Boys Academy in Vancouver, Washington.

8

"FOXY LADY"

I wanna take you home
I won't do you no harm, no
You've got to be all mine, all mine
Ooh, foxy lady
                    Sung by Jimi Hendrix

I didn't know I had been "sexually abused" until I had been
married for over ten years and had three children and was
in therapy for relationship problems, because of compulsive
and addictive behaviors.

The therapist was a female colleague who had graduated
from the same university from which I was seeking my
doctorate. As she probed into my past to help identify
possible root causes, I told her about my first sexual
experience, with the thirty-five-year-old woman when I was
just barely fourteen years old. She asked if I remembered
any details or feelings from the event. I told her the vivid,
detailed memories of the initial encounter leading to the first
moments in the bedroom. I related the excitement and fear
that I felt when my behavior and requests to her most likely
gave away my total lack of experience and childish ideas.

The therapist immediately declared that I had been
"sexually abused" and further that I was most likely a victim

of post-traumatic stress disorder as evidenced by my fear and subsequent memory loss after the initial event in the bedroom.

I protested that I had certainly not been raped or molested. I had been a willing (though terrified) participant; the woman thought I was older because I told her so; and I kept going back to the house all week long. I also shared that when I told others (mostly men) about it, they said that I was "lucky" and that they envied my experience.

Then my therapist asked a question that changed my viewpoint forever: "What would you say to a woman in counseling with you who at barely fourteen years of age was taken into the home of a thirty-five-year-old man for a week of repeated sexual experiences? Would you say that she had been sexually abused?" "Of course," I replied, "but that's different." "You bet it's different," she said. "Most boys of that age are much less emotionally mature than girls are, making it possibly even more traumatic." She continued, "What behaviors might your client exhibit following such an event?" Together we listed several possibilities, including:

- repetition compulsion (where the victim may seek to repeat the experience often with an older person)
- promiscuity or frigidity (depending on her mindset at the time)
- inability to have normal relationships with members of the opposite sex her own age
- fear of intimacy

- feelings of guilt and self-blame (particularly if she was willing or enjoyed any part of the experience)
- dissociative episodes (in which she may "block out" past or present activities)

The list went on into other comorbidities too numerous to mention.

My therapist then asked if I had experienced any of these problems, and I had to admit that I had been plagued by most of them for years. She repeated, "You were sexually abused. What part of that do you consider as 'lucky'?"

As I reflect back on that experience, I am aware even now many years later of how difficult it is to face the impact of being sexually abused. It is still difficult to accept the concept.

In our society, there is a double standard by which we view the sexual experiences of men versus women. As a man, I am supposed to be proud of my sexual prowess and exploits; I am supposed to be the initiator, while women choose the individual with the strongest presentation of manhood. Women are often seen as victims, not perpetrators, especially when it comes to sexual abuse. I am not supposed to identify with women as having been victimized. After all, I was the one who led her into the entire experience ... or was I?

What would have happened if I had said to her upon entering the car, "Hi, I am a very troubled fourteen-year-old ninth grader who has never had any sexual experiences of any kind, and further am terrified that I might do something wrong or that I'm not good enough, so would you please drink booze with me, keep me in your house for a week, and show me everything about sex that I couldn't possibly learn any other way?" She would have probably stopped the car and thrown me out.

I was obviously hiding my true self as I had already learned to do so well on the streets. I was good at hiding. I always hid the fact that girls my own age thought something was wrong with me. I was too tall and old-looking for a young teenager; I was unfriendly (because I didn't have a clue how to relate to them); I was dumb and did poorly in school—quite a "catch" to bring home to meet the parents.

It's certainly true that my self-image was already damaged by the physical abuse from my stepfather and the rejection from my biological father, who was no longer my "dad." Now, however, I thought of myself as a complete failure who would never have a normal "relationship" with anybody, let alone a member of the opposite sex. I found my survival mode worked best when I "faked it."

For many years, I sought out brief impersonal sexual experiences with older women. Many of the occurrences did not even reach a sexual point. My subconscious drive was to prove to myself that I was a "real man" who was not afraid of my inability to perform or my feelings of not being wanted by anyone.

I use the word *subconscious* because I didn't admit any of this to myself until many years later. By the time my therapist had introduced the concept of "sexual abuse," my life had begun to spiral out of control, almost to the point where my ability to "fake it" was in danger of complete and total exposure.

In therapy, I began to deal with my fear of women. I had often chosen more permanent relationships with women who were strong in their morals, had little or no experience like mine, and were able by their very lives to show the glaring reality of my own inadequacy. I, of course, did not show any of this in my initial courtship, so they were obviously shocked when the "hidden" side of me began to emerge. I was fearful that they would judge me, condemn me, or expose me, and thus I was able to perpetuate my own self-image as a failure that didn't belong in their world or anyone else's.

I am certain that much of my hiding was necessary for my survival in the traumatic environment on the streets, as a runaway, with the first woman, or similar subsequent experiences. However, it is the nature of post-traumatic stress disorder to continue survival tactics long after they are no longer needed—in fact, continuing to perpetuate them when they serve no purpose other than to be totally dysfunctional.

༄

For many years, I had been considered the "problem child" in my family and by many who knew me in a social or vocational context. Without question, many (or most) of my problems were only because of my own extremely poor choices. Many persons, counselors, and mentors had told me that I had no one else to blame except myself when I was dysfunctional, and I believed they were right.

However, *Blame*, like his twin brother *Shame*, usually produces more self-condemnation than self-liberation. Having a context in which I could understand some of the roots of my self-destructive choices was very liberating. I began to see the cause and effect of my actions, which enabled me to change the impact of those choices at the "trigger point" rather than after the "explosion" had become devastating. I love what Louis L'Amour wrote:

> *Up to a point a man's life is shaped by environment, heredity, and movements and changes in the world about him. Then there comes a time when it lies within his grasp to shape the clay of his life into the sort of thing he wishes to be. Only the weak blame parents, their race, their times, lack of good fortune, or the quirks of fate. Everyone has it within his power to say, "This I am today; that I will be tomorrow."*

I needed to take responsibility for my own actions, as everyone does. But often abused children don't know at what point they lost their way. It is most helpful when lost in the woods to retrace your steps to find where you first got off track, rather than walk in circles trying to find a "new" pathway out.

Getting on track is not easy, because many of us have spent a lifetime trying to hide our subsequent behaviors and choices, and have often reached the conclusion that we are "bad to the bone" as the song describes. But it is my belief that while we may act that way, we are NOT that way, as evidenced by our conduct when given the opportunity to nurture a child or help others along their own pathways.

Self-awareness and willingness to be open with others are essential to engaging in the change process. Mark Twain said, "Everyone is a moon, and has a dark side which he never shows to anybody." Nowhere is that more true than to victims of child abuse who often believe they cannot show their "light" side to anyone either.

In *Hamlet*, a father tells his son, "To thine own self be true, and it must follow as the night the day, thou canst not then be false to any man."

But, are self-awareness and openness to others *enough* to break the patterns of behavior a victim has engaged in as a result of the trauma that was inflicted upon him or her? *Absolutely not!*

We have to deal with the addictive nature of the repetitive actions that we utilize to bring the trauma back upon ourselves. The truth is that we grow to love our self-debasement. Our self-destructive thoughts, plans, and actions become our new identity, because they promise to relieve our pain.

I am not aware of many persons who after having been hit with a hammer addictively seek to relive the experience. However, many who have been hurt in a variety of ways seek to bring punishment upon themselves by engaging in behavior that is terribly destructive to every aspect of their lives ... simply because it feels good for the moment.

⋙

Speaking of the moment, can we take a break? All this self-awareness stuff makes me want to take a nap.

"Just stay with me. This isn't easy to do, but it needs to be said."

◌

If we are truly going to look into ourselves, we have to get *real* about the things that we don't want to give up, because even though we know they are bad for us, we love them too much to let them go.

In the book *The Velveteen Rabbit*, the rabbit has a conversation with the wise old Skin Horse:

> *"What is real? Does it mean having things that buzz inside you, and a stick-out handle?"*

"Real isn't how you are made," said the Skin Horse.
"It's a thing that happens to you."
"Does it happen all at once?"
"It doesn't happen all at once. You become. It takes
a long time. That's why it doesn't happen to people who
break easily or who have sharp edges, or have to be
carefully kept. Generally, by the time you are Real, most
of your hair has been loved off, your eyes fall out, and
you get loose in the joints and very shabby."

The rabbit sighed. He thought it would be a long
time before this magic called Real happened to him. He
longed to become Real, to know what it felt like; and
yet the idea of growing shabby and losing his eyes and
whiskers was rather sad. He wished he could become it
without these uncomfortable things happening to him.

Most of us also want to "become it" without working
through the pain.

To get real with yourself is always difficult. But it is the
only way to get healthy, especially if your primary coping
skills are pretending and hiding.

I want to be "true" to my own self as Shakespeare
advocates, but it is surely a long and painful process. I know
that I must often choose to *stay with my pain* and learn from it,
rather than seek to run away.

The lessons from the streets are powerful if I will only pay attention. The failures they have brought are my only key to true wisdom. But I didn't know any of this at the time I was placed in the Vancouver Boys Academy and "Slimy Slim" came back into my life.

9

"THE GREAT PRETENDER"

Oh yes I'm the great pretender
Pretending I'm doing well
My need is such I pretend too much
I'm lonely but no one can tell
Sung by the Platters

The Vancouver Boys Academy was located in an old military building on the east side of Vancouver, Washington, which was across the Columbia River from Portland, Oregon. The academy, or "VBA" as we called it, was a private Christian program in which the juvenile court placed me but didn't pay for. My mother paid the entire cost (over a period of years) because my father didn't have any "extra" funds; he probably had neglected to tell her of the probation officer's prediction or the fact that he had "given up" on me anyway.

The building had two long wings with offices and a gymnasium in the center. On one wing were the dormitories and some staff quarters, while the other wing held the cafeteria and classrooms. Both wings were connected by a long hallway down which you could see all the way to the end, from one wing to another.

I would eventually become very acquainted with every inch of this long, wooden hallway as I was often assigned the task of cleaning, waxing, and buffing it on a daily basis. The metal buffer was so heavy it took two strong guys to lift it. It was probably responsible for my determination to not become involved in heavy lifting or manual labor as a future vocation, if I could possibly help it.

When I first arrived at the VBA, I was assigned to a dormitory that had about twelve to fifteen guys in it. The academy had about forty to fifty residents (ages twelve to eighteen) in total, in four different dormitories. One was an "honor" dorm, which I was fairly certain I would never see, and the others were categorized according to age, size, and availability.

I was placed in Dorm #2, which I thought would be my home for the rest of my life. As I noted before, I wasn't really suicidal but didn't see a future of much length, either because God would give up on me as others had or because some genuinely tough kid would see through my facade and beat me to death some dark night behind the horse barn.

The academy grounds were fairly extensive and had a pasture for several horses, a softball field, and a small wooded area with trees at the far end of the pasture. The woods became a place of refuge for me—after I had been in the academy long enough to be trusted enough to disappear for a while.

I had a tough time adjusting at first and ran away at least a couple of times. One of those times I ran away with a kid named Jim. We decided to run just after bedtime one evening, with a plan to hitchhike to the Oregon Coastal Highway, and from there head all the way to Mexico.

We had a great time for the first couple of days. We told people who picked us up that we were on a sightseeing trip just before going to college and that we wanted to "live a little first." By the second night, however, our vacation plans changed. A rainstorm moved in, and we got soaking wet. We found a bus stop that had a wooden structure with a roof and front and back sides to it, but it was open on both ends.

As we huddled together freezing, hungry, and wet, we talked about what it would be like if we were back at the academy. We imagined having eaten a great meal in the dining room. We even laughed about wishing we were there to do chores after dinner, although I wasn't certain that I would want to do dishes even if it did mean that we would be warm.

The next morning, we decided that freedom wasn't all it was cracked up to be, and we turned ourselves in to the police in the northern California town of Crescent City. We were put in a jail cell, but we were given food and stayed warm.

The next day, as we were preparing to be transported back to the academy, I started thinking about the trouble we would be in when we got back and also wondered if they would even take us back. I felt the weight of discouragement again as I talked to a police officer. He asked me what I thought could be gained from running away, and also what I was planning to do with the rest of my life. I told him that I thought it would be better for me if he took out his gun and shot me to end it all. I felt that old familiar feeling that I had once again messed up my life beyond repair. Instead, one of the academy staff came, and we were taken back to the academy.

I was surprised that they were willing to take me back, and even more surprised when the staff reassured me that they thought I might have a positive future, and further that they believed in me.

I was none too happy, however, when they still disciplined me for the serious infraction of the rules. First they made me bend over and grab my ankles, and they gave me several "hacks," as they called them. A "hack" was a really hard smack with a long wooden paddle. It really stung like crazy, and even the toughest kid couldn't make it past three without crying. Five hacks were the maximum, and that was the usual for "running."

The second discipline was much less painful physically but had the greatest impact emotionally. They shaved our heads with electric clippers after we returned from any run that lasted overnight. This was during a time long before a shaved head represented anything "cool," and going out in public, for a group activity or to church, was humiliating.

It certainly served the purpose of discouraging running away for the reason mentioned, but it also really hurt the self-image. As a young man who was deathly afraid of being seen for what I actually was underneath, being seen physically as a "total geek" didn't help much.

What did help were the staff as a whole and especially certain ones in particular. There was Ron, a very sharp single guy in his early twenties. He went to college and lived in the staff quarters across the hall from the dorms. He could have done anything and lived in any place of his choosing because he was confident, very bright, and destined for greatness, but he chose to give his time to a bunch of difficult, troubled teenagers because of his commitment to a higher calling to serve others rather than use his gifts and abilities for personal gain alone.

He was also the basketball coach. I am certain that he saw in me a six-foot-six young man with absolutely no talent or athletic ability at all. Ron was way too sharp to have missed the obvious, but he never told me. He nurtured me (bottle-fed is more like it) as a member of the VBA team from the beginning of my stay there to the end (one and a half years). I became the starting center, though I must have had a vertical jump of about six inches. But as I put on more weight, Ron trained me to get in the way of agile opposing players and to block the shots of those who were a foot shorter than I.

Membership on the VBA basketball team also probably kept me from getting beat up, because it gave me some status in the social hierarchy of the group.

Ron later became the executive director of the Vancouver Boys Academy and the founder of its successor, Youth Outreach, Inc. This became a group home program renowned for its innovation in community-based treatment for troubled youth. He also later became one of my primary mentors, which was a task at least as difficult as teaching me to jump high enough to touch the rim of a basketball hoop—in other words, nearly impossible.

There were also many other inspirational staff at the academy, but I have to mention the primary teacher who dedicated the latter part of his career to our education. We simply called him "Aarhus," which was his last name. I don't remember his first name, but I remember the "Doctor" in front of his last, and it was never my intention to demean him in referring to him by his last name only. In his presence, he was "Dr. Aarhus," and he forever set the standard for that title in my mind.

Whenever someone refers to me with the title of doctor, I have only to think of him and I immediately realize how far short I am of such an honor. He was the most intelligent, learned, gifted, talented man I have ever known. He was also the kindest, most sensitive, and gentlest person, and he taught me that a real man doesn't have to put up a "macho" front. He was the most "real man" I have ever known. I still have psychology books in my library given by him, as we talked about the possibility of my pursuing a career that might someday utilize them. They are among my most treasured possessions.

༄

While the staff at the academy were inspirational for the most part, my fellow students were equally as deleterious. They were mostly like me. We were often engaged in some kind of subterfuge, with plans to bring in forbidden pleasures like "dirty" magazines, booze, or tobacco products.

The one thing that most of us had in common was the desire to impress others, without the ability to correctly see how others viewed our "stories." We would share with each other the amazing details of exploits, which always seemed to be even more amazing because we all knew that they couldn't possibly be true.

We talked about the impressive mechanical skills that we had as we described major engine rebuilds that we had put together on shiny Impalas and 1932 Ford Coupes and a host of other cars with multiple carburetors, chrome pipes, and amazing speed records. Of course we never saw any pictures, but that didn't stop the embellishments that were generated as one kid after another trumped the lies of the last one to speak.

Another source of unbelievable stories was our prowess and connections with girlfriends and other women who followed us around hoping to be chosen as our next amazing experience. I, of course, could have shared the truth about the thirty-five-year-old, but I was always troubled when I thought about the whole thing. Besides, it was just easier to talk about the fantasy women that I knew so well in my mind, especially when my "girlfriends" were better, richer, more attractive, and hotter than any of the made-up women that my fellow "liars" could ever describe.

The real truth was that if any of us actually possessed any of the cars or women or experienced the successful exploits described, we would not have been in the academy in the first place. Most of us were there because of family or legal problems to which we had responded very poorly, causing one failure after another. The academy brought us together, but most of us just fed off the lies and troubles of each other, rather than using the experiences as a wake-up call to get our lives together.

There was Dave, who insisted that he regularly smoked a pipe (like Hugh Hefner), which really made him "cool." He also played the bass fiddle in a jazz bar in Portland (which made him more adult than I could ever be). Dave also talked about drugs (which I had not yet tried), and we were all convinced that he could put out a "contract" on us at any time with his "underworld" connections. He was probably seventeen years old at the time.

There was Bart, who didn't have to do anything to look or act older. He was already balding and shaved twice a day. He was a weight lifter who was meek and quiet ... with deadly venom lurking just below the surface.

There was "crazy Mike," who walked around with wild-looking eyes and an evil grin most of the time. He was skinny but wiry and strong. He once held up a chair over his head and threw it at Bart (of all people), splitting his lip open. Then crazy Mike ran screaming down the hall toward the office. After that episode, we usually gave him a wide berth when passing him.

Then there was me. A tall, uncoordinated basketball player who couldn't use the judo master disguise anymore because of the disastrous consequences, so I became "Slimy Slim" again.

❧

What? Who wanted to be Slimy Slim again? Boy, talk about not learning from your mistakes.

"I'm not saying that I was proud of it. It was just my identity at the time."

〜

I left a few details out in the telling of my heroic experiences, such as knocking the crap out of that sixteen-year-old in the county jail in Salem, but I showed the scar on my lip from having to fight the twenty-four-year-old to defend my honor. My rendition worked so well that I painted the inscription

"Slimy Slim" on the back of my leather jacket, like the title of an outlaw gang member.

I started lifting weights and wasn't so "slim" anymore with the starchy academy food, and with my voice becoming deeper all the time, I started developing a tougher image. My new identity worked well enough to encourage further hiding of my fears and I got along all right at the academy.

What didn't work was my getting any closer to the healing I so desperately needed to ever become a productive member of society. The problem was not the academy's treatment of troubled kids. The problem was that many of us weren't ready to own up to our poor choices and would need a lot more personal failure before we would "wise up."

The academy was a good influence for most of its residents and planted seeds that would later come to fruition in remarkable ways.

During my stay at the VBA, I had a lot of positive experiences that began to change my self-image. I started doing better in school, because I began to hope (if not believe) that I was capable of doing good work. I had spiritual experiences, which seemed to give purpose and meaning to life, and I discovered a sense of peace that often calmed my troubled mind. I even had a few opportunities to just be a kid, with group activities including swimming, camping, and other "normal" kid stuff.

But when I went home to Seattle on home visits, I still maintained my connection to the streets. As often as possible, I went downtown to skid row. I liked to immerse myself in the "life" of the city and pretend that I was still the adult who was free from all responsibility and the demands of society.

As I prepared to leave the academy for the last time, I knew that I couldn't keep up the facade of being a well-adjusted high school student whose future was bright. I truly missed my accelerated adulthood in which my teenage problems were gone and I could move on with the life of fantasy that I created as the street kid.

At the end of my tenth-grade year, having been at the academy about a year and a half, my mother took a new job in Helena, Montana, and I was released to go with her and my little sister, so all of us could get a "fresh start."

Helena, Montana, was wonderful … for at least five months. The news of my arrival spread quickly through the high school community shortly after the summer began. They had heard (somehow) that I had been the "starting center" for a high school basketball team in Washington State. I was immediately accepted by the "in" crowd of popular kids who were looking forward to my performance when the season began in late fall.

Unfortunately, they didn't realize that my "performance" began the day I arrived and would end when the season started. In the meantime, I was enjoying my fresh start. I dated some of the popular and most attractive girls in town. I hung out with the popular athletic guys who had parties at my house (when my mom was gone), and most important, I had a wide variety of friends—and lots of them. Life was really great.

When school started, I turned out for football, but it was determined quickly that it was not my sport. I only made the B squad and didn't play much, even though I was six foot six and now weighed about 245 pounds. If no one looked too closely, I still appeared pretty "lean and mean."

The basketball coach met me and worked me out a couple of times. He saw that I was a bit rusty, but he was a nice guy, very encouraging, and told me that with practice (which I didn't find time for) I would "really shine."

When the season opened, my cover was blown. I was on the team for a couple of games but was only a junior, and the senior center was awesome, so I never played. I was soon kicked off the team for drinking, which I admitted as soon as it had become known, and saved a little of my reputation because I didn't have to show the absence of any real skill.

It was decided that I would return to the Vancouver Boys Academy to finish my junior year because I couldn't face the rejection caused by my charade. The basketball team welcomed me back, especially when they found out (somehow) that I had played for a big school in Montana. I went back to standing under the basket on defense, blocking the shots of small opponents on the church league that we played in.

The Helena High School newspaper that year honored me with mention in the section of songs that best fit the honoree. Mine was "The Great Pretender."

I returned to Helena for my senior year. But when I turned seventeen, I quit high school and joined the navy.

∾

10

"LOVE ME TENDER"

Love me tender,
Love me long,
Take me to your heart.
For it's there that I belong,
And we'll never part.
Sung by Elvis Presley

"Love" and "belonging" are two of the primary human needs as listed by Abraham Maslow, who is renowned for his development of the "Hierarchy of Needs." This was true for me; I desperately needed to be loved and to belong ... somewhere. I just wasn't going about meeting the need in the right way. Just at the point in human development, as a teenager, when I should have experienced "my friends" as more important than almost anything else, I didn't have any. I am fairly certain that, even in Helena, I would have been liked and accepted if I had only been honest about my inability in the athletic arena. I just didn't know how to be honest, because the main thing I was good at was hiding and "faking it."

Over the years, as a therapist who often worked with troubled youth in residential treatment settings, I encountered many kids who were like me as a teenager.

Most of them really needed to feel loved but were almost completely unable to receive it when offered. Many of the kids in group homes and other treatment environments had major trust issues with the adults in their lives.

The caregivers in these residential treatment settings, like the staff at the Vancouver Boys Academy, were mostly motivated by a strong desire to help troubled kids work through their problems and become good, productive citizens in the future. The problem was not the well-intentioned caring staff but the severity of the abuse and trauma that contributed to the youths' distrust of ANYONE'S attempt to provide that care.

Instead of receiving the love and care that they so badly needed, many of the teenagers pushed it away with an intensity that was difficult to comprehend. As a result, many staff became frustrated, exhausted, and disappointed when the interventions they worked so hard to provide were completely rejected. Most caregivers have the greatest difficulty continuing in their heartfelt efforts in the face of that which seems to be a personal attack upon their entire mission and purpose for working with these kids in the first place.

As a therapist and teacher, I suggest to prospective caregivers that one of the most important elements of working with others who are hurting is to memorize and practice DTIP:

DON'T TAKE IT PERSONALLY.

꩜

As I attempt to remember the "shut-off" feelings of being a troubled youth, I know that it would not have made any difference what interventions were offered to me; I was too discouraged and isolated within myself to allow the love to shine through. The street kid inside me pushed every attempt away, even though what I truly needed was someone to understand and to keep trying, and trying, and trying.

As a teenager, I spent over two years in the Vancouver Boys Academy. The program eventually worked in forming and shaping my life. However, it was a long time coming.

My mother received a letter from the academy when I was about twenty years old, part of a follow-up study. She was asked how I was doing, and she responded, "It's too early to tell ... ask me when he's thirty."

At the age of twenty, I was still allowing the impulses of the street kid to dominate my life. At the age of thirty, I had experienced a major life change. I had finished my bachelor's and master's degrees and had returned to work at the Vancouver Boys Academy (now called Youth Outreach, Inc.). My mother knew something that escapes a lot of well-meaning caregivers: the work is not in vain, but it may take years to blossom ... and the caregiver may never even be aware of the results.

To be a caregiver to troubled youth is a most noble profession, and it needs to be done wholeheartedly, without regard for a specific outcome, because every effort given has the potential of a ripple effect to touch many others in the future.

In residential treatment, as in parenting, marriage, friendships, etc., the primary value in offering real meaning comes as *relationships* are developed. Many programs for youth offer a wide variety of interventions that are designed to change negative behavior. For example, behavior modification systems motivate change by working toward earning an external reward. The desired behaviors are reinforced because the youth strives for the reward, thus acting in a more acceptable manner. Progress can be charted, and change in the behavior actually happens. In fact, most residential programs see significant changes in the behaviors of even severely troubled youth … as long as the structure of the program is maintained, and the resident can see the immediate benefit of participating in the program.

Behavior modification works to produce *external* change, as the youth works to gain an *external* reward. It doesn't become *internalized* unless something happens to change the self-image, the self-control, the trust issues, and a host of other problems that are buried deep inside.

❦

"Wow, that sounds intense. I love it when you sound professional … and doctoral!"

"Since when do you like that language? Usually you kind of put it down, like it's not important, or real."

"C'mon, Doc, I know it's important ... and real. Just try not to sound too stuffy!"

༄

Internal change—*real* change—is brought about by having relationships with people who genuinely care for you, and for whom you care enough to want to change yourself as you emulate them.

I don't remember the specifics of treatment interventions or of the service delivery system in the academy. But after I began to allow some of my self-esteem to improve, I began to feel that some staff members genuinely cared for me, which planted seeds to suggest that I might be actually *worth* caring for.

Relationships work best to influence change when instead of *telling* someone how to change, we *show* them how we allowed change to happen in our lives ... and encourage the same in them.

Many persons who want to become caregivers to others, without seeking help for themselves first, sometimes labor under the delusion that if they help others, they won't have to look at their own stuff. One of the main problems with that concept when working with troubled kids is that the street kid inside can see right through it. The street kid can spot a "phony" from a mile away.

The truth is that if we want to effect change in others, we first have to pursue that change in ourselves. If that hasn't happened, we can only offer solutions that have worked for others but of which we personally know nothing.

The best caregivers, whether parents or teachers or therapists, etc., are those who have learned from their own failures and experiences, and are willing to be open and real about themselves in order to form genuine relationships. Many observers ask if they need to have similar experiences to those whom they want to help. The answer is: of course not! They just need to know how to face their own stuff and be *real* about it.

This is not to say that they have to self-disclose every failure, because they need to place the needs of others above their own, but if they can't even admit *some* areas of their own problems, how can they hope to ask others to do so?

Of course, learning how to be in a real relationship begins with those we *should* be closest to in our own lives.

∽

I had an experience with my daughter, Amanda, when she was fifteen years of age. She had gotten into some trouble and as a result was in a hospital program. I was invited into a family session in which Amanda begged me to remove her from the hospital setting, but I told her that I would not.

She then screamed at me, "If you are going to leave me here, then why don't you just leave my life right now? You always run away ... so just leave me alone!" At that point, I allowed my *feelings to get hurt* and left the session, leaving my daughter behind.

The emotions that flooded my mind allowed the street kid to burst onto the scene with self-destructive thoughts and intentions that I had not experienced in a long time. My first impulse was to "go back to the streets and leave it all behind," but while that may have worked in the past, there was no way that I could leave my daughter with the impression that *she* was responsible for my self-destructive action.

I called her the next morning. In tears, she asked me why I left the session. I replied, "Because you told me to go." She responded, "Daddy, I may have told you to go away ... but I didn't *want* you to!"

I burst into tears and told my beautiful daughter that "no matter how hard you temporarily push me away, I will never leave you again." I then asked her to forgive me, which she promptly did.

This incident brought Amanda and me closer to each other than would have ever been possible otherwise. It worked because even though Amanda was the one in counseling, I still had to own my stuff, choose a better way of handling it than allowing my feelings to be hurt, and be open and vulnerable in order to further our relationship. In doing so, I once again experienced my own change process, which will continue throughout my life, if I remain open and do not run from it.

∽

Owning my stuff requires that I engage in some honest soul searching.

In my private counseling with patients, I inform them that the most therapeutic tool that I have in my office is the "Magic Mirror." As people are encouraged to look deep within themselves by looking into the mirror, they are often uncomfortable with the self-image that their real feelings reflect back to them. Like all of us, they need to be honest with themselves in order to make real changes.

Facing the truth is contrary to the way that most of us have learned to deal with our feelings of inadequacy and our own experiences of pain. The street kid runs away from pain and sabotages relationships and any resemblance of success, whether real or imagined. Asking the street kid to quit pretending, to look honestly within, and to be open to engage in the change process is frightening. There are so many places within that are left behind on purpose.

As Thomas Harris states in his book *HANNIBAL*:

> *But this we share with the doctor: in the vaults of our hearts and brains, danger waits. All the chambers are not lovely, light and high. There are holes in the floor of the mind, like those in a medieval dungeon floor ... nothing escapes from them quietly to ease us. A quake,*

some betrayal by our safeguards, and sparks of memory
fire the noxious gases ... things trapped for years fly
free, ready to explode in pain and drive us to dangerous
behavior ...

The street kid urges nonconformity to most of society's
expectations: avoid responsibility; let sleeping dogs lie; leave
the feelings buried; and above all, forget your pain and move
on with your life. But the truth is that feelings buried alive
just don't die. We have to confront our deep, secret fears
and failures if we are ever going to get better enough to even
think of helping others.

When I quit high school to join the navy, I was still
running away as hard as I could from the biggest failure of
all ... *myself.*

11

"A CHANGE IS GONNA COME"

I was born by the river in a little tent, oh
Just like the river I've been runnin' ever since
It's been a long time comin', but I believe
A change is gonna come!
Sung by Sam Cooke

I signed up to join the United States Navy and "see the world." I was filled with the hope that my troubles were also being left behind because I was on a fast-track to finish my high school education by correspondence courses, obtaining my GED, or by some other method that I had not quite figured out. I was also fairly certain that because this move would thrust me into the "real" adult world, I wouldn't have to pretend anymore ... I could just *BE* who I was.

I wasn't quite sure if they allowed dropouts to achieve the rank of admiral, but I figured that an exception could be made once they recognized my true potential.

Five months later, I went AWOL (absent without leave). It wasn't that life on board ship wasn't exciting (I was assigned a mop and bucket to "swab down the decks"), but I just gave in to an *impulsive moment* while at a house party in Balboa, California. My new best friend suggested we take his "new" used car up Route 66 to St. Louis, Missouri. What an adventure!

❧

"Here we go again."

"What?"

"Why do all adventures have to start out in chaos?"

"No pain ... no gain."

∾

When we got to Flagstaff, Arizona, the car (a Jaguar sedan) quit runninvg, and my friend suggested we leave it by the side of the road with a note that said, "Thanks for the test drive, but I've decided not to buy at this time." Realizing that the vehicle was stolen, I agreed that we should put as much distance as possible between us and the car, so we started hitchhiking.

We were surprisingly successful in getting good long rides, and other than spending a couple of nights sleeping in a ditch alongside the road, we made the trip safely.

Once we reached St. Louis, the first thing that happened was a major breakdown in communication with my traveling partner, and we decided to go our separate ways. It seemed that he thought I wasn't serious enough to pay attention to the task of survival because I was always looking for something fun to do with my time. He even said that I was "childish"!

My venture into the real adult world wasn't working as well as I had planned, so I fell back to my old ways and faked it. I got a job selling encyclopedias door to door, bought some clothes, and settled in for a new career in high volume, high income sales.

The impulse hit me again two weeks later. I hitchhiked to Houston, Texas, because that's where my ride was headed. After a few days, in a brief moment of clarity, I decided to turn myself in and go back to the navy. I had been gone for twenty-nine days.

I was given a special court-martial, busted all the way down to E-1 (from E-2), and spent two months in the brig at the U.S. Naval Air Station in Corpus Christi, Texas. In the brig, I learned new ways to improve my communication skills. I became able to rattle off my requests so fast and unintelligibly that only a marine guard (or "jarhead") could understand them.

"Sir, prisoner Cecil requests permission to speak to the inside turnkey, sir?"

"Grunt."

"Sir, prisoner Cecil requests permission to enter the cellblock, sir?"

"Get in here, boy!"

This communication style was imprinted on my brain so that I would never forget it—I'm glad that I've never had to use it again. *One time* in a navy brig with marine guards is enough to last a lifetime—I hope!

On the train back to San Diego with orders to report to a new ship, I thought, *What am I doing here anyway? Three years ago, I was homeless on the streets. Now I'm a dropout busted to the bottom and headed back to swab more decks. How long ago was it that I was at Helena High School? Weeks? Feels like years.*

That's my old life. I need to forget my old life. I've got more important things to think about ... that girl in the lounge car was pretty cute. I wonder if she would like to go on a date when we get to San Diego. I better tell her I'm a naval officer. That will be great. I can't wait to take her out. Boy, if the kids at Helena High could see me now, I bet they would wish they were here enjoying this freedom. It doesn't get any better than this!

๑๛

Two months after arriving on board ship, I fell twenty feet down a cargo hold, spent six weeks in Balboa Naval Hospital, and was discharged on a medical because I was "too tall" for service on board ship. The doctor made me promise to go back to high school. At least I got veterans' benefits.

I went back to Helena High and (barely) finished my senior year.

In returning to Helena High School, I was fairly well accepted because I now possessed a new worldly adult knowledge that got me by ... most of the time. At least no one suggested that I play basketball, and I was free to pursue my real passions.

I was aware of a secret yet powerful longing to seek connections with women much older than I, and that seemed to make being in an "honest" relationship with girls my own age much more difficult to fake. I, of course, didn't tell anybody about the thirty-five-year-old woman in Seattle—or any of my secrets.

∽

One evening, shortly after I returned to Helena, I was parked down the street from the RB Drive-In watching the traffic go by when two girls pulled up next to me in their car. It was dark, and I was pretty sure they didn't know who they had pulled up next to.

I thought, If I lean over and roll down the window, they will see that it's me and drive away laughing. I wish I knew who they were ... then I could fake it better by laughing at them. Who cares? They're just silly little girls. I'll just ignore them. Sure enough, there they go ... laughing.

At that point in my life, I'm certain that I didn't understand the phrase "a self-fulfilling prophecy."

Later a girl told me, "A lot of girls want to ask you to the Sadie Hawkins [female initiated] Dance, but they're afraid you will turn them down." I couldn't help wondering what they would think if they knew that I was terrified of rejection, but no one would ever know.

Within a year, I would be homeless and penniless on the streets of Seattle … again.

~

I had been living in Spokane for a few weeks. A distant relative of my father's, Rev. Cecil, was a minister, pastoring a large congregation in the city. He had seen my "potential," so he bought me a suit and helped me get an apartment and a job selling shoes. I was once again back on the fast-track to success.

If only I hadn't had that *impulsive moment*.

I met a guy with a "new" used Impala convertible, and while we were cruising for chicks one evening, he suggested that we might do better in Seattle. We decided to "go for it," and I went back to the apartment, packed all my stuff, and we hit the road.

In leaving a note for Rev. Cecil, my mind was full of contradictions:

> *Dear Rev. Cecil:*
> *Thank you for all your help. An opportunity*
> *has come up which requires my immediate presence*
> *in Seattle. I look forward to talking with you again*
> *sometime in the future.*
> *Ric*

I hope the apartment manager gives him the note. He is such a nice guy. I wish I could explain it to him. I guess I'm not quite ready to settle down ... I'm not sure why, I just know that I've got to go!

The next morning, my new best friend and I were cruising through a residential neighborhood in Seattle at 4:00 A.M. looking for a hose with which to siphon some gas. As I searched a nearby yard, a police patrol came around the corner, so I hid behind a car in the driveway. When I emerged, the patrol car was gone—so was my friend with everything I owned, including my trombone. I never saw him again.

I went back to skid row, but while everybody *looked* the same, nobody actually *was* the same. I hustled some money by telling a modified version of my friend's abandonment, and I rented a room at the YMCA in downtown Seattle.

I reverted back to my old ways of hustling in order to finance my new adventures and started hanging out in the numerous bars and gathering places on Pike Street. Pike Street was in itself a place of adventure. The Pike Place Market, with its cobblestone street, was at the west end with one-way traffic headed east past the strip club on the left and the donut shop on the right at First Avenue. The street was filled with taverns and cafés, department stores, Woolworth's variety store, and a host of other businesses including jewelry stores, shoe stores, banks, and theaters.

Often I hung out at the market, which offered several levels of shops and food stands, and a lot of places to sit and watch people (as long as you didn't hang around too obviously because the beat cops might start asking questions about your identity and purpose for being there).

Most of the time, during the day, I stayed farther up the street at Larry's Greenland Café, on Pike and Eighth, or at the Outer Limits Tavern near the Kansas City Steak House on Pike and Sixth Avenue. At night, the real action was at the Caballero Dance Tavern, just down the street from the Greenland.

The "Cab" had a pool table near the front with money action going all the time. The dance floor was back by the band's stage, and the live band was hot and played R&B songs. That was the first time I heard Sam Cooke's last song "A Change Is Gonna Come."

I kept feeling that my "change" was surely just around the corner and that my potential would soon be realized.

∾

I met her on the corner in front of the Coliseum Theatre.

She was good looking, well-dressed, and in her middle to late thirties. She told me that she thought I looked "interesting" and wondered if I might be someone she could talk with about her problems. She said that she lived up the coast in Edmonds with her husband, but they had no relationship. She wanted to "help" me and took me shopping for clothes.

After a few weeks of clandestine meetings at prearranged places, we finally got a room and "did it." I guess I wasn't what she had envisioned or something, because after that we had some disagreement and she left me standing on the corner. I never saw her again.

I thought, Who cares! It's all just a game ... I'd rather be by myself anyway. I'm not going to feel bad just because some rich chick can't use me anymore. I think I'll go bum some money and get some fish and chips at Ivar's, and feed the seagulls. Maybe I'll stop in and see the twenty-foot jawbone of the hundred-foot sperm whale at the Ye Olde Curiosity Shop. I'm going to have a good time! It doesn't get any better than this!

It didn't get any better for a long time.

~

The next few years are just a blur. I was often caught between a new awesome job and an impulsive moment. My main area of expertise remained my ability to pretend to be an adult, but I felt like a *thirteen-year-old*.

I was still pretty good at faking it, so I gravitated to sales. I sold pots and pans, shoes, vacuums, sewing machines, and pianos. My impulsive moments took me from Seattle to Montana to Yakima, Washington, to Hollywood, California, to Portland, Oregon, and many points in between. I don't know how many cheap hotels I stayed in, how many street people and pool hustlers I hung out with.

I became a bouncer and bartender in a nightclub, worked in a fast-food joint (for at least three days), and generally worked really hard at doing nothing. I wound up becoming what I had always imagined myself to be ... a failure.

I didn't know it then, but the street kid continued to live inside me. At any moment he could get scared, or feel unable to pretend anymore, or get his feelings hurt by something real or imagined ... and dominate my life with impulsive choices and hazardous behavior.

12

"I CAN SEE CLEARLY NOW"

I can see clearly now, the rain is gone,
I can see all obstacles in my way
Gone are the dark clouds that had me blind
It's gonna be a bright (bright), bright (bright)
Sun-shiny day.

Sung by Ray Charles

Eventually I left the streets, but they never left me. I kept them alive because part of me was still the street kid, and always will be. The street kid influenced a lot of my choices and decisions, but I didn't really identify him until I began to "wise up" from the repeated consequences of the impulsive moments.

My experiences on the streets taught me *survival*. The skills that I gained in reading people quickly to see their true intentions and how to get enough money to find a warm, if not safe, place to sleep, etc., were skills that often transposed into valuable assets as I grew into adulthood. On the streets, these lessons kept me safe and helped me to escape the confusion and abuse of further trauma in an already dysfunctional family system.

The self-image that developed within me served to make me often more comfortable with chaos and failure than with harmony and success. As a result, my inner self impacted my thoughts and motivations in much more self-destructive ways than I could ever imagine.

The hustler inside was always looking for "action," thus the street kid continued my lessons long after I spent my last night in the *safe haven* of skid row in Seattle.

I found that I didn't know how to *play*. The things that helped me to escape were mostly dysfunctional. In addition to my primary addiction of wanting to run away, I became involved in a variety of escapes: gambling (especially in pool games that re-created the "nurturing and safe" environment of the pool halls and skid row taverns); illicit drugs (stimulants gave energy, while sedatives offered refuge from the self-induced maelstrom that my agitated mind and behavior created); and sex (not the act of lovemaking that fosters true intimacy, but seeking to repeat the experiences of my own victimization, with older women with whom I could expect no *real* intimacy or relationship). The street kid was often beckoning to go play ... he just didn't know how.

One of the major consequences of being thrust into the pretend adult world was the *loss* of my adolescence. Instead of learning how to relate to teammates or fishing buddies or best friends—to share insecurities, perplexing curiosities, or hopes and dreams with others—I just became further isolated within my troubled and alienated mind.

I had no context in which to relate to others except in the world of the "misfit." I fit into the culture of the streets and pool halls and skid row bars ... I still do. But I didn't fit into the sophisticated, refined society or the professional community because I felt that I couldn't be *real*.

This is not to say that there are no genuine people in those roles, but I just didn't know how to relate. I found it difficult, if not impossible, to make small talk or stay at a surface level when sharing on most topics in social settings. It was just easier to show the rebellious, oppositional, delinquent teenager—the street kid—to keep others at arm's length rather than admit that I longed to be accepted and not rejected anymore.

∞

While the street kid made it hard to fit in with others in a professional or social setting, I found it much different as a family therapist. As I attempted to help others with their problems, I found my own experiences to be well received, useful, and valuable. Parents called and said, "Do you have any openings? I have heard that you work well with oppositional kids, and my teenage boy is falling apart. The last counselor told me that there is no hope. Do you feel that way?"

I found that sexual and physical abuse victims often felt they could trust sharing their stories, things they had never talked about with anybody, after they heard a little of my own background. Adult children of dysfunctional families seemed to relate to the chaos and confusion about self-image and self-destruction especially in relationships. Of course runaways and those who felt like failures sought me out to explore their impulsive actions and the resultant, often disastrous, consequences.

I found that being real was something that most struggle with, and they seek options that actually work, rather than just stir the stew of their lives by rearranging the ingredients. Like me, most sought counseling to gain enough *self-empowerment* to QUIT PRETENDING! The willingness to stop pretending is the *key* to opening the door to a wisdom that is not available to those who have not experienced repeated failure.

∽

The streets have produced a learning experience of great value that I could not have gained any other way.

On one hand, the conflict raging inside me drew me toward a defiant masculinity in portraying myself as a rebel who would *never fit in,* and didn't want to. On the other hand, I felt softly drawn to a self-awareness that whispered that I would become *real* only if I acknowledged my feelings and let them mold me into a gentle, sensitive man who was not afraid to realize and be open with that sensitivity.

Native Americans refer to a *good* warrior as one who is both gentle and strong but to a *great* warrior as one who knows when to be which!

As my *self-esteem* and *self-control* grew stronger, I began to see the deeper *wisdom* that comes from searching for *harmony and balance* between the opposing forces rather than constantly running from one extreme to the other.

When we descend too far into the dark, we can't function anymore. When we transcend too far into the light, we are blinded to the reality and meaning of our own growth experience.

∽

Of course the greatest value of any wisdom is the impact that it produces not only in our own lives, but in the lives of those who have been placed under our care. Nowhere is that more true than with our own children.

In our society, the children of the helpers and caregivers are often sadly neglected as the shepherds leave their own flocks to tend to the compelling needs of the *others*. But what is the *cost* of caring for others if we have lost sight of those who need and depend on us the most?

My own four children became the driving force behind my efforts to fully appreciate and utilize the lessons and experiences of my tumultuous adolescence. Each of them is actively engaged in the wonderful life process of simply becoming themselves. It is the only thing I truly desire for them. I don't want them to be a copy of me in some way. I don't want them to choose a vocation or life's work by what I might choose for them. I don't want them to become something that I could not so that I might live vicariously through them. I just want them to BE who they ARE—to think for themselves and follow their own paths.

❧

Shortly after Clint, my first child, was born, I was watching him sleep through the nursery window at the hospital. I wondered what our relationship might actually be in our future. *What if he doesn't even like me? All kids are supposed to love their parents, just for being parents ... but will he really love me once he finds out who and what I really am?*

Suddenly, I knew the answer: *Of course he will. Just be the kind of father to him that you always wanted for yourself!*

❧

Amanda, my only daughter and the youngest of the children, as a little girl used to say to me, "You like to spend as much time with us as you can, because your daddy didn't spend time with you ... huh, Daddy?" I responded then (and now) by saying, "That's right, honey. I *love* spending time with each one of you!"

A couple of years ago on her twenty-first birthday, she asked me to accompany her to get her first tattoo. The design she picked was a shoot of bamboo. This was significant to her because I called her "Amanda Panda" when she was young and pandas eat bamboo. Even in adulthood, Amanda wanted to celebrate her childhood in part because she *knew* that she was loved.

She even invited me to join her, with siblings and friends, to celebrate the birthday by going out on the town. I don't know how many fathers are invited to a twenty-first birthday celebration, but I believe it is a rare and esoteric opportunity enjoyed by a chosen few.

As I remembered the example of my preacher cellmate in the county jail, which I always tried to emulate, it was my tremendous privilege to attend the celebration, and even the street kid got to let loose a little!

※

"Yeah, it's about time! Since you've been into all this harmony and balance stuff, I hardly ever get a chance to 'go for it'."

"Well, I do have to admit we had a good time. With a little balance, you can actually be fun!"

"Thanks!"

∾

Clint, my oldest son, was athletic and always a member of one sports team or another throughout his childhood. I tried to attend as many functions, games, and road trips as possible, even though I lived a hundred and fifty miles from where he lived with his mother and the other kids.

On one particular trip, when he was in the fifth grade, his teammates went into a store to stock up on goodies for the trip. Clint and I had gotten our supplies earlier, so

I suggested that we remain in the car. At this suggestion, Clint stared at me in disbelief and said, "Dad, let's go be with the guys!"

Clint continues my social development each time we are together. We play pool (he is *much* better than I), and he keeps me focused on how to relate to others in crowded settings in which the street kid is often alienating and looking at others with suspicion.

❧

Brian, my youngest son, was most vulnerable at the age of four when the children's mother and I ended our marriage of fifteen years. He was very bright and sensitive, and often covered his feelings of loss and hurt with rebellion and anger, especially in social settings.

His relationship with me was not well defined, and he often felt lost and uncertain about himself and where he *fit* in the family. But he always talked to me about his problems, and as we both grew emotionally, we began to share a lot of our mutual insecurities and anxieties.

Today, Brian is perhaps the closest of all my children to me when I need to share feelings of confusion or failure. In being open with him, I know there will be no judgment or even disappointment. I know that Brian loves and accepts me *just the way I am*. And I feel exactly the same toward him and all my amazing children.

❧

Eric, my middle son, called me a few months ago from New York City, where he lives and studies classical guitar as a full-time student in a music conservatory. He related that he had been talking with a classmate about the influences that have shaped their lives, and Eric told him, "You've got to meet my dad. He has done *everything*, including messing up a lot. But he has taught me that it's not whether you mess up, but whether you get up afterwards and learn from your failures, so as not to make them as often in the future."

Then Eric said to me, "Dad, I told him that *you* were the most positive influence in bringing me to the place I am today." He paused and then said, "Dad, I just wanted to call you and thank you and tell you that I love you and I AM PROUD OF YOU!"

I thanked him for calling, told him, "I love you too" (which the children and I often say), and then hung up the phone and burst into tears.

What an amazing reality! A rebellious, oppositional, delinquent teenager who was a dropout, a failure in his own mind and life, could be so successful in the greatest and most challenging assignment and task that life affords—a close, open, and *real* relationship with his children!

∽

13

"PHASING"

A classical composition by Eric R. Cecil
"Phasing" is an improvisatory guitar piece, which I've played for
many years. The essential harmonic progression remains the same,
which I use as a template to introduce new techniques and musical
ideas. Thus, it is always the same piece, yet it is new each time,
constantly undergoing a transformative process, which reflects my
musical and personal growth.

Opening this chapter with my son's words is a phenomenal
privilege. When he describes the musical piece as "always the
same, yet new each time," reflecting his own "musical and
personal growth," it becomes a metaphor for life.

Life is such an incredible journey. If we will only embrace
the traumas and tragedies, faults and failures, together with
the positive moments that breed confidence and success, we
will realize that each event has the potential to revitalize our
lives as we learn and grow from every experience.

I did not spend the rest of my life behind bars as the
probation officer predicted when I was thirteen. Without
question, many of my choices *could* have propelled me toward
a pathway that fulfilled that prophecy. However, many
other choices have led me along a journey that is fulfilled

by turning my liabilities into tremendous opportunities to enrich my own, and others', quality of life.

Criss Schlaht, a friend who has worked through his own wisdom process, says, "Instead of a liability, our failures have become a tool." However, the tool is only an instrument of unrealized potential, until it becomes an extension of the skill in the craftsman's hand.

For many of us, the awareness that we have something to offer as skilled craftsmen requires a lot of trial and error, failure and defeat, before we can allow the realization that we *are* able to overcome, and it is primarily the lessons of our failures that make this possible.

Becoming aware that we have not only overcome our failures, but also learned that we can help *teach* others is the beginning of a wisdom that comes only from failure—"The Wisdom from the Streets." The greatest truth from that wisdom is: *If somebody like me can do it . . . anybody can!*

It all begins with becoming strong enough to allow the truth to shine through, knowing that no matter what the failure, or trauma, or choices that bring devastation, whether self-inflicted or not, the moment that we choose to get healthy and become *REAL* with ourselves, the path toward self-empowerment is under our feet immediately.

A change *is* gonna come . . . and will continue to emerge as long as we incorporate the process into our lives.

As a therapist, I love working with rebellious, oppositional, defiant children and teenagers. I remember what it felt like to be labeled all of those things. I also remember the sincere but misguided counselors who tried to relate, but usually left me feeling that I was hopeless and alone, with no one who really understood my pain and conflict.

It is often said that people in the helping professions choose their areas of interest based on their own unfinished business from their conflicts of the past. This is most certainly true for me. Many troubled teenagers whom I have worked with express a desire to help others with their problems. Even in the midst of their own struggles, they still have a tendency to be available to friends and associates in trouble. Often we feel as though there is *no one* who can relate, so we turn to others in similar situations who can at least give a perspective from their own experiences, whether successful or not. However, being able to just *relate* doesn't really help much until they have learned enough from their own failures to offer some guidance toward a new pathway out.

For me, simply relating to the world of the street kid is only helpful if I connect with the lessons, so that my counsel to others actually offers something of value for their own journeys.

It has been said that "the greatest tragedy of all is to have lived through the experience, but to have missed the message!"

As I continue to work on my own self-discovery process, the *true messages* come through:

- Learn from your failures.
- Don't dismiss them as experiences to forget and leave behind.
- Embrace the lessons as growth opportunities.
- Learn (and practice) new ways of coping.
- When failure comes anew, don't get down on yourself; get back up and keep growing.
- Share your progress and principles for growth with others who can learn to embrace their own process.
- Remember that you are not alone. Many have come through similar problems successfully. Seek them out. You will know them by their lives, by the way they treat others who are in pain and feel like a failure, by the absence of judgment and condemnation they display, because their own "glass houses" do not allow for throwing stones.

∾

As a therapist, I relate to the world of the misfit. However, I have to be cautious that I don't alienate others whose experience is different than mine. There is much to gain from those who have not failed as I have. I just have to watch my tendency to put up a barrier between us because I feel that I can't trust them with the *real me*.

Personal growth means that I not only accept myself, but *all* who are engaged in their own struggles, and provide for them an atmosphere of warmth, caring, and acceptance, as I listen to the telling of their own stories. As they begin to share their pain, the most important thing that I can offer to them is to show them that I am also struggling and be real enough to expose the personal vulnerability of my own conflicts.

When I get *real* with myself, I can offer my true self to others. Self-disclosure is not a technique for use in therapy; it is an essential element of forming a relationship with those who need to know if they can *trust* enough to expose some of the dark and secret places within themselves.

The issues of the street kid are the focus of my own healing process and also the help I give to others. I offer the following as insights regarding those issues.

∾

PARENTING

Our *goal* as parents should be to help our children achieve independence and the belief that they can reach forward to all the potential that life affords, regardless of any limitations or circumstances.

The two most important elements they need to achieve their own dreams are:

Self-Esteem and Self-Control

As parents, we must use every opportunity to help our children *feel good about themselves*. In the middle of *any* interaction with them, we need to ask ourselves if our actions will enhance or detract from their *self-esteem*.

The easiest way to accomplish that is to *treat them the way we would like to be treated*. Even though our parents often did the best they could, if something did not *feel* right to us as children, it may not have *been* right, and we need to treat our children accordingly.

We also need to use that same rationale when we consider the things we will allow them to do on their own. Of course we want to protect them and keep them from harm, but we must not keep them from situations that will produce learning that they can safely gain *on their own*.

As they grow older in preparation for their own entry into the adult world, we must allow increasing freedom for our children to make decisions of their own choosing. If we can foresee difficulty or even failure on the horizon, we must not intervene until they ask us for our help to guide them into *self-control*.

We also must:

Be a Resource

If we have allowed *trust* to develop in our relationship with them, we will serve them best by being a *resource* when they seek *wisdom* from our experiences, rather than dominating them simply because we, as parents, pretend to know the right answers. We often *don't* know and need to tell them so.

෴

RELATIONSHIPS

Relationships with others are often dysfunctional because we desire that they serve to meet *our* needs, and when that doesn't happen as we expect, we are disappointed, wounded, or even angry. However, rather than simply expecting that others will always act in a way that does not hurt us, we need to take responsibility for *allowing* ourselves to be wounded by our own expectations, which are often unrealistic.

Relationships (with children, family, friends, significant others, etc.) work best when we:

Own Our Stuff

by refusing to blame others for our own dysfunction and woundedness. People who own their own stuff get better. People who don't become bitter. To own our own stuff doesn't mean that we are the problem in the relationship and the other person has no responsibility. But if we blame others, we allow their behavior to dominate our thoughts and blind us to the only thing we *can* change—ourselves.

Get Real with Ourselves

by admitting to ourselves that we cannot change others with anger or assaults, presents or promises. We can only work on changing ourselves within the relationship. If others refuse to work on themselves, we may need to leave the relationship, but even leaving requires that we get healthy enough to change.

Encourage Reciprocity

not by a conditional response (I will scratch your back *if* you scratch mine), but by a *mutual* decision to engage in being supportive to each other in the change process.

෩

ADULT CHILDREN OF
DYSFUNCTIONAL FAMILIES

Those of us whose lives have been negatively shaped and influenced by being raised in a dysfunctional family need to recognize that a *healthy* family is *not* one without problems, but one in which the members are *honest and open* with each other about *any* problems.

Functional families need to:

Break Dysfunctional Generational Patterns

by recognizing that "the way we always handled things in our family" may *not* have been the right or best way to handle them, then or now. Secrets, myths, alliances, guilt trips, etc. must be honestly *examined* and *discarded* if found to be hurtful or unrealistic.

Be Willing to Start Over

Even if Uncle Buck or Aunt Bertha strongly advocated a specific way of doing things, we must be willing to find a *new way* if the old one no longer works for us. Sometimes the best option is to cut our losses and begin again.

෩

PERSONAL FAILURES

Our own failures are either great tragedies or tremendous learning experiences. The *choice* is ours. If our *self-expectations* are such that we can only accept perfection, yet do not believe that we can achieve it by any means, we set ourselves up for constant failure. Striving for an unattainable perfection keeps us *stuck* in a self-destructive mode. Instead we must:

Change Our Viewpoint

We may have allowed our *attitudes* to be self-destructive and our viewpoints to be self-defeating. But we *can* and *must* view our failures as *enrichment* experiences, which *strengthen* and enable us to *overcome* any obstacle.

Don't Do Guilt

Feeling bad about our self-destructive actions will *never* allow us to move forward. Guilt will only place us on a never-ending *cycle* that continues to spiral downward into a bottomless pit. We must *learn* from our actions, take *responsibility* for them, and *change* our response in the future.

◈

RUNAWAYS

Pretending and *hiding* are two major characteristics of the runaway. Pretending that our "old life" doesn't exist anymore helps us leave behind the things that propel us toward our escape. Hiding keeps us from discovery. It serves to keep others from finding out where we are, either physically or emotionally. We can run away without even leaving home.

We can run to the "streets" of our own choosing and often develop a pattern of leaving behind the things we just can't face—in our relationships, our jobs, our finances, or whatever *seems* to be the *source* of our pain and confusion.

However, the source is usually deeper or simply different than our perception of it. Rather than running from an event or a circumstance, we are often just running from ourselves. Thus, we eventually discover that instead of *getting away* from it all, the problems are waiting for us when we either reach our destination or retreat back to our starting point.

Pretending and *hiding* are almost always dysfunctional responses when running away. Instead, we need to:

Search for Alternatives

To run away is usually not the best or safest option. We need to find *resources* that are able to really address the underlying issues rather than *pretend* that our response will take care of us or protect us. There are always avenues available that we haven't tried. We just need to look for them.

Embrace Self-Discovery

Even if we are afraid that we won't be good enough or smart enough or that others will disapprove, we must look veraciously at ourselves. Discovering the truth about who we really are will only facilitate our personal growth and offer direction to guide our pathway toward our greatest potential.

∽

VICTIMS OF PHYSICAL, SEXUAL, OR EMOTIONAL ABUSE

Children usually blame themselves for the abuse and chaos brought into their lives by others. As a victim of abuse, I understand that we often see the results in our own lives in the subsequent actions that drive us to self-destruction, when we see no other option to escape our troubled world. Our self-image and confidence are shaken to the very core of our being. As a result, we remain as children, regardless of our chronological age, until we begin to glimpse the light that beckons us to a new genesis that will re-create our lives.

Our minds often provide a defense mechanism that blocks out the trauma, as we *dissociate* our awareness of the abuse and go to a place of forgetfulness that allows us to cope with our circumstances by numbing the pain. The dissociative process builds upon a subconscious attempt to stabilize a trembling foundation.

Our misguided efforts to cope with our victimization seem to have little value in the real world, and the truth is that we need to:

Celebrate Our Survival

We have proven to the world that we will *not* succumb to the wounds, but we need to begin *believing* it for ourselves. We must *affirm* our *conquest*.

Learn to Trust Ourselves

Our trust has been shattered, but we need not be hypervigilant toward all others with the *fear* that they will continue the *victimization*. We can trust our *instincts*. We can trust our *intuition*. We can trust our *decisions* and our *choices*. That which was done *to* us does not have to *define* us. Once we learn that we can trust *ourselves*, the pathway will *NOT* be driven by the wounds of the past, but by the present, which *empowers* us to fulfill our destinies.

∞

The *lessons* that produce *wisdom* are often the result of life experiences that are driven by the desire to run away from *pain*. Most of us try to avoid the feelings of rejection, hurt, sadness, conflict, or whatever is distressing to us.

But, as in the physical realm, all *pain* serves a major function in the healing process because it is often the primary indication that something is wrong and needs our undivided attention.

Anger may cover our hurt feelings, but we need to *stay with our pain* long enough to learn from it, before we explode into actions that make the situation worse. Thus the *pain* continues our lessons by offering many opportunities for personal growth.

If we will only pay attention, the *wisdom* available will produce amazing results that enhance every aspect of our lives.

∞

Recently, as I was leaving Chicago on a westbound train, I saw a tragic message that had been spray-painted on a wall. It read:

"KIDS LIKE US WILL BE ALONE FOREVER"

When I saw it, I thought, *But it doesn't have to be that way.*

"Kids like us" just need someone who has learned enough from his or her own journey—and cares enough to reach out with the truth:

> There are those of us who have also felt that way and want to help guide you into a new life where you will never really feel alone again.

My journey as a runaway used to be the defining characteristic of my life as a "failure." Today I view that journey as a lifelong process that continues to be one of my greatest assets as I attempt to pass that wisdom along to others.

The conflict inside, the subsequent failures, the desperate soul searching, the strengthening of my self-esteem and self-control, and the desire to reach out with simple yet profound insights for others in pain have become the realized progression of my true self as I continue to embrace the lessons and "Wisdom from the Streets"!

AFTERWORD

When people hear some of my story, they usually ask, "What was it that turned you around in the first place? How did you decide to go in a different direction and start helping yourself and others, instead of being self-destructive as a failure?"

The answer is that I experienced a spiritual awakening that stopped me in my tracks and resulted in a whole new set of *impulsive moments* that produced a lot more chaos—and wisdom—than I could ever imagine.

But that's a whole different story that deserves another telling.

THE CONFLICT CONTINUES

«Can I say something about the book?»

"Sure, it's about you."

«Well, not entirely ... it's about you too, isn't it?»

"Right. I should say it's about us. But, what did you want to say?"

«Well, it seems really good ...»

"But?"

«Well, are you going to tell the story? Are you going to tell about the things that happened after the time period of the book? You know, the major change that turned you around in the first place ... and then ...»

"And then *you* responded like an illegal cherry bomb on the Fourth of July?"

«And what about you? It seems that you tried to take us down the `primrose path' leading to more disaster. Are you going to get real and write about that? I think you need to write another book, starting at the end of this one.»

"Good point. I do need to talk about my religious conversion, and my efforts to take the 'higher road,' and my 'fall from grace,' and my troubled relationships, and a lot more failures."

«And the drug scene? Boy, that was a trip.»

"Sorry, but I know that if I am going to encourage others to be real, I have to be willing to tell the whole story."

«Come on, it'll be fun. I'll tell you more street kid stories.»

"Okay, you win. It happened one time when I was on the run and …"

Made in the USA
Charleston, SC
10 August 2010